Here's what people are saying about Susie and Otto...

Praise for Susie and Otto Collins' No More Jealousy . . .

"We're definitely impressed! We don't think we've ever seen a
book or course anywhere with as many rock solid and specific
tips, suggestions and strategies for overcoming and eliminating
jealousy as Susie and Otto Collins' *No More Jealousy.*"
--Paul & Layne Cutright
Best Selling Authors of *You're Never Upset for the Reason You
Think* www.youreneverupset.com

"*No More Jealousy* saved my relationship. With your help, Roger
was able to let go of his unwarranted fear that I would abandon
him and we began to have a healthy relationship . . . without
jealousy . . . thanks"
–Kathi Zahniser

"*No More Jealousy* changed my life. I saw extreme jealousy in my
father and hated the way he treated my mother because of his
unfounded fears. However, I found myself battling the same
demons and mistreating people in my own relationships.
"I found *No More Jealousy* online and ordered the program. After
the first few chapters, I found myself understanding my feelings
and for the first time in my life, dealing with my jealous tenden-
cies instead of reacting to them. It has given me tremendous
freedom. Thank you for your great insight."
–Robin Farmer

"The day I purchased your book was the start of a much better life for both of us. Through reading your book *No More Jealousy*, Hazel and I have become aware of what has been triggering some of the feelings that we have experienced from time to time. Understanding this has enabled us to know how to handle these feelings and we have started to communicate on a new level. Your book has helped us enormously since reading it."
–Rod Anderson

"Thanks so much for your book about jealousy! It has given me the confidence to step out of the mold I had created for myself. Finding your book came at a time when I needed it most. Thanks again. A very helpful reference."
–Trudy Woodward

"Since reading *No More Jealousy*, I find that I'm much slower to react when I feel threatened."
–Jack Kavanaugh

"I was very pleased with *No More Jealousy*. It made me feel a lot better and see things differently. Now if I feel jealousy, I just read the book and my jealousy goes away."
–Antigoni Vagelis

"*No More Jealousy* has proven to be an extremely useful tool for me. It has helped me to center my thoughts and actions if I feel the fears coming on associated with jealousy. It was helpful to understand what jealousy really is, and with that knowledge and the exercises offered in this program, I feel I am much better at handling my insecurities and fears."
–Karen Westerfer

No More Jealousy

Breakthrough Strategies and Insights for Overcoming Jealousy and Creating a Better Relationship Now!

Susie and Otto Collins

Conscious Heart Publishing
Chillicothe, Ohio

Table of Contents

Acknowledgments

We are very grateful to all of the contributors to this book who so willingly shared their stories with us and gave us permission to use them in the hopes that their words will be helpful in your struggle with overcoming jealousy.

We would like to acknowledge and appreciate all of our teachers who have helped us to learn about relationships and personal growth, especially Dr. Belinda Gore who taught us the "Power of Presence" exercise and much more.

We would also like to thank Peri Poloni for the cover design and Janice Phelps for interior design.

Introduction

If jealousy is an issue for you in your relationships and in your life, we don't have to tell you how painful living with this issue can be.

If left unchecked, jealousy has the power to destroy otherwise wonderful relationships (sometimes without a clue as to what went wrong).

Not only can jealousy destroy your relationships, but it can also keep you from getting promotions at work, create embarrassing scenes in social situations and, in general, keep you from having as much peace, love and joy in your life as you would like.

Sometimes people who have jealousy as an issue in their lives tell us... "I don't know why I feel this way. I guess I'm just the jealous type."

What we've discovered is that no one is born to be the "jealous type." There are reasons why jealousy is an issue for you in your relationships.

It's our intention in writing this book to share with you exactly what these reasons are. We'll also help you discover what jealousy is, what causes it, how to recognize it as quickly as it comes up and to give you some strategies for letting go of it when it does come up.

In this book, you'll read the jealousy stories of several people. These are stories of pain and triumph. Even though we've withheld their names for privacy reasons, we'd like to thank them for sharing what jealousy has meant in their lives in the hope that their stories will give you courage, strength and the feeling of possibility that you too can overcome this issue.

When you're able to let go of the jealousy, you'll be on your way to deeper, more connected and more fulfilling relationships as well as a better life, free of constant drama, fear and anxiety.

About us and our challenges with jealousy . . .

We've been teaching people how to create great relationships since we came together as a couple several years ago after the break-up of our previous marriages. We had known one another casually because we were members of the same spiritual study group in our town, but the intense attraction and soul mate bond didn't happen until after we were single again.

When we got together, we knew the type of relationship that we wanted, and we began to practice what we had learned about relationships over the years. People began to notice that we had something special and asked us for advice, and to give workshops. We received training to be coaches, created websites, wrote books, and create audios with the intention of helping people create the relationships of their dreams. A passion for our own relationship, plus helping other people, is our purpose for doing this work.

We share what we have learned from our hearts with hope that you can use it to enrich your life and your relationships.

Both of us have struggled with jealousy in very different ways and that's why we feel so passionate about sharing what we've learned about it with you.

Susie's story:

"I was married for thirty years to a man who was a good husband, but I was mistrustful of him from time to time. I would become very agitated and sometimes almost in a panic when he was late or at a conference, although there were no outward signs he was being intimate with other women during these instances. As the years went on, we lived congenially but we began living our lives separately to a greater and greater extent. The glue that had held us together just began to dry up.

"In the last year of our marriage, I became suspicious that he was becoming very close to another woman who shared one of his hobbies. He began spending evenings in the upstairs of our home, much of the time on the phone. Since I paid the bills, I noticed the long distance calls that he was making and put two and two together. When I asked him about the calls, he admitted what was happening with the other woman. We took several months to mutually decide to divorce after seeing a counselor and many long talks.

"When Otto and I got together, he gave me absolutely no reason for having jealous feelings, but I found myself having them anyway, at times. I found that I wanted his attention all to myself. In certain situations, it was difficult for me to be with him with groups of people, especially women. I found myself getting jealous when he was involved in an intense conversation with someone, especially with another woman. I couldn't explain where these feelings were coming from, but I knew it would destroy our relationship if I didn't heal the underlying cause.

"The difference between my experience with my ex-husband and my experience with Otto is that I knew that the jealousy issue was a problem and I was willing to face it. I was willing to work on myself and change the direction of my thinking. What you'll read in the following pages is much of how I have healed and continue to heal those wounded parts of myself that were showing up as jealousy."

Otto's story:

"I've discovered that jealousy isn't just about mistrusting a partner who you think is having an affair. Jealousy can be manifested in many areas of your life.

"For me, I haven't been jealous of who I've been in relationship with. I've never really worried about who my partner was talking to, whom they were friends with or what's going on with them and the other people they worked with or came in contact with. I figured they either wanted to be with me or they didn't and if they didn't, there wasn't a lot I could do about it since that would be their choice too.

"What I have felt jealousy over is money.

"For you it could be something totally different.

"When we got together, Susie and I made agreements about how we were going to handle money, because we each had sources of income and separate obligations. There are three different types of 'money' in our relationship-Susie's, Otto's, and ours-and I found myself becoming jealous of Susie's savings and monthly income from sources other than our business.

"From time to time, I have become jealous not just of Susie, but of other people who had more money than me, had a better job than me and even people who held better community or social positions than I did.

"What I realized was that this had nothing to do with money, jobs or positions in society or life, but it had everything to do with what was going on inside of me.

"As I started going underneath my jealous feelings about money, I discovered that I was jealous because up until that time, I hadn't been able to create the financial stability in my life that I wanted, and there was a fear that I would never be able to. I also feared losing what I had."

This is what we've discovered about jealousy: It's almost never just about the jealousy itself. It's about whatever is underneath the surface of your jealous feelings.

Making the Commitment to Change

One thing we know from our experiences and from the experiences of our clients is that the first step to changing anything in your life begins with making the commitment to change.

We are firm believers in the idea that action follows intention and thought. Before you read any further, we invite you to examine what you are committed to and to entertain the possibility of making a commitment and setting the intention that you are going to create the kind of life that you are wanting.

When you make that commitment, especially if it is in writing, you set the stage for changes to happen. Without opening to the possibility that you can change, it's likely that you will stay stuck in the same patterns that you've lived with for perhaps many years.

If you are ready to begin making the changes that you need to make so that jealousy is no longer an issue in your life, we invite you to write that commitment below:

I am committed to . . .

_____

_____

_____
_____

_____

Did any doubts come up for you as you wrote your commitment?

_____

What we've found is that it's very common for doubts to come up when you're thinking about a commitment like this.

If you're like many people, you might have heard an inner voice in the back of your mind saying negative things to you as you wrote your commitment.

Your commitment may have been something like...

"I am committed to being open to making the changes that I need to make in my life so that jealousy is no longer an issue."

And the negative inner voice may have said something like...

"BUT I've never been able to do it so far," or *"I'll never be able to really do it!"*

If this happened to you, write your doubts below:

_____

_____

_____

_____

_____

_____

_____

To assist you in your process of letting go of jealousy more quickly and easily, we invite you to do two things:

1. Write out your commitment on pieces of paper or small cards and put them in prominent places around your home, office and car—wherever you will see them. You might put one in your purse or pocket, any place where you will be reminded frequently of your commitment.

2. As you read and work through the rest of the material in this book, we invite you to acknowledge your doubts but not let them hold you back in changing your life and healing the jealousy in your life. When doubts come up, we suggest that you say to yourself something like the following: "Thank you for sharing, but right now I'm choosing to believe that I can heal jealousy and have the life I want."

With this in mind, let's take a deeper look at what jealousy is.

Chapter 1

What Is Jealousy?

We'd like to begin by describing what we think the term "jealousy" *isn't* and then share with you what we think it is.

First we'll begin by sharing with you what we call the "Seven Myths about Jealousy."

Seven Myths about Jealousy:

Jealousy Myth # 1

"Jealousy is only one person's problem in the relationship."

Although one person may be showing outward signs of jealousy, both people are involved in the "dance" that's going on between them and also in the healing process. We will explain what we mean in Chapter 4.

Jealousy Myth # 2

"If we just get married, his (her) jealousy will disappear."

Many people believe that marriage will be the cure-all for anything that is wrong with their relationship. One person may have a "feeling" that there are some traits about the other person that they don't like in a partner but ignore that feeling.

They have the belief that they can change the behavior of the other person after they are married. This simply isn't true. People do change but no one changes unless they want to.

Jealousy Myth # 3

"If we have kids, he'll (she'll) settle down and we can become a family."

If anything, having children actually puts more stress on a relationship and oftentimes brings out our worst traits.

Although bringing children into this world is certainly a blessing, it does not mean that expanding your family will stop damaging behavior. What it usually means is that this behavior will escalate, and it will have to be dealt with.

Jealousy Myth # 4

"If we don't talk about it or look at it, it will go away by itself."

People live their entire lives with this belief.

The truth is, whatever it is won't go away until it is named, dealt with and healed. Many of us have been taught to be "nice" and not say anything that will "hurt" the other person. But— what many others and we have found— is that the truth bubbles up later, often in ways that are more damaging than if the problem had been faced openly.

Jealousy Myth # 5

"Jealousy only shows up in intimate relationships. It doesn't cross over into other parts of your life."

Jealousy can and does show up in all parts of your life. As you read the stories in this book, you'll be able to see how the fear that is underneath all jealousy tends to show up in other parts of your life.

Jealousy Myth # 6

"If she (or he) weren't so beautiful or attractive, jealousy wouldn't be an issue."

Although a beautiful partner can attract more attention than an average-looking partner, if both people are secure in themselves and in their relationship, jealousy will not be an issue.

Jealousy Myth # 7

"I can trust her (or him) but it's the other people that she (or he) comes in contact with every day that causes me to be jealous."

This is a big one-especially jealousy surrounding co-workers. We strongly believe that no one is "lured" into an attraction for another person. There is usually something lacking in the relationship-something that the person is looking for-that fosters this attraction for someone else. We believe that attention to the relationship is the best "cure" for this one.

We've just talked about the seven myths of jealousy and what jealousy isn't. Now let's spend some time exploring what jealousy is…

What Jealousy is . . .

Marianne Williamson says, "Everything we do is either an act of love or a cry for help." *The Course of Miracles* says there are only two emotions: love and fear.

It's been our experience that fear of one kind or another is underneath all jealousy. Jealousy is about real or imagined fears-fear of abandonment, fear of loss of love, fear of being dishonored in the relationship, fear of being shamed in the community, unresolved issues from past relationships, lack issues, poor self esteem, a cover or mask for things from the past that you haven't healed yet, a desire for revenge that is misguided or misdirected toward someone else.

When jealous feelings come up, it's usually because we're afraid that we won't get our needs of one kind or another met. It's been our experience that when jealousy comes up, somewhere within us, we are crying out for help.

Jealousy seems to be expressed in a couple of different ways with a partner:

1. The first is when there is "proof" or at least a strong suspicion that agreements and commitments between two people have actually been broken by one of them.

2. The second way jealousy shows up is when one or both people in the relationship are very insecure in their relationship or in life. Jealous feelings come up with a partner, or others, whose actions haven't warranted it.

Whatever is going on-whether the jealousy is "warranted" or not-fear is at the bottom of those feelings and there's a lot more going on than what is on the surface. What we've discovered is that until we look at those fears and begin to heal them, no matter what relationship we're in, jealousy will creep in again and again.

An example of how fear can make you do crazy things . . .

One Saturday night in late spring, early on in our relationship, we had been out shopping and were on our way to meet some friends for dinner. The very simple act of finding a parking space turned ugly as quickly as you could snap your fingers.

We were in an unfamiliar part of town and we didn't realize that the parking lot where we had parked was about to close. We realized that if we wanted to stay in the area and have dinner with our friends, we were going to have to move the car to a different parking spot.

It didn't seem like parking spaces were going to be easy to find, but when we could see that a space opened up across the street from the parking lot we were in, we wanted to grab it for ourselves.

Big problem. We were not in our car at the time. As Otto walked to the car, Susie decided to physically stand in the parking space until he could park the car in that space, which would only be a couple of minutes.

It wasn't sixty seconds until someone else pulled up to the parking space (where

Susie was standing) and started backing her car into the space. As the woman continued backing her car, it didn't appear that Susie was paying much attention to what was happening. Either the driver didn't see Susie or the woman wanted the parking spot so badly that she was willing to run over Susie to get the parking space.

When Otto saw that Susie didn't realize that she was about to be run over, he instantly became enraged. By the time he got to the parking space, Susie had moved and the woman had parked and gotten out of her car.

Otto confronted the woman, becoming more and more upset with each passing moment. This woman and her young son began to walk away. Otto began following her, then finally came to his senses.

This situation involved similar dynamics as to what happens when jealousy arises toward another person.

Otto became upset when he saw this woman nearly running over Susie with her car. But, what was underneath his anger was a deep sense of fear that if this woman continued doing what she was doing, Susie could have been killed. At least that was how it was in his mind in the moment.

When we examine this truly bizarre scenario deeper to see what was really going on, we find that what caused Otto to react in the way that he did was fear that his relationship with Susie was jeopardized by a woman wanting a parking spot.

From a practical standpoint, Susie did realize that a car was backing up and if she didn't move, she would get run over.

But in that moment, Otto's irrational mind became so filled with fear and rage that nothing made sense and he quickly lost control and made the whole thing bigger than it needed to be, as he realizes in retrospect. In that moment, however, his reaction was very similar to the reaction of a person who is experiencing jealousy.

It's not rational, it doesn't make any sense, the situation isn't really "real" and it probably isn't something the jealous person thinks he/she can control.

Fear of loss, especially loss of love, can cause some people to exhibit some very strange conduct.

To give you an even deeper understanding of what it's like and how painful it is for some people when jealousy comes up, let's consider the following descriptions expressed by some of our former clients about what it's like for them when they are feeling the emotions and feelings of jealousy (all names have been changed):

Carol has a problem with her second husband who is a doctor. She becomes jealous when he's in an examining room alone with a woman. What happens to her is that she gets quiet and doesn't talk. That has caused problems because the quieter she gets the madder he gets. She feels he doesn't care about her as much as he does his patients. She feels unimportant and unloved. He doesn't understand where this jealousy is coming from and she realizes that her withdrawing is pushing him away even further.

Suzanne has been seeing this man for three months and is suspicious because she never sees him on a Saturday night. She thinks he might not be dating her exclusively. When her fears get the better of her, she gets quiet, turns off her feelings and becomes numb. Where she might have felt loving toward the person, she turns very cold and that creates tension between the two of them.

Joy went through a divorce and is recently remarried. She and her husband have a good relationship but she is jealous of the relationship her husband has with his ex-wife. She keeps her feeling inside; she doesn't think her jealousy is healthy. She knows she needs to trust her husband, because she feels that he would never do anything to violate their commitments to each other.

Carl wants to learn to trust again. His previous relationship ended when his partner had an affair and left him. Since then, he's had a hard time trusting women and he's nervous about being hurt again.

Joe's jealous feelings are uncontrollable and he ends up lashing out at his wife. He knows that he is the problem but when the feelings come up inside him, feelings that are embarrassing, he knows he needs to stop but finds it impossible to let them go.

Christine's challenge is a trust issue. When she gets in a relationship, she tends to get paranoid, unsure of herself and begins to take on the role of a victim.

In their descriptions about their jealousy challenges, these people talk about "withdrawing," "getting quiet," "becoming numb," and "lashing out." All of the behaviors that these people are describing are all ways to shield, protect and insulate themselves from the pain they are feeling inside themselves.

The approaches they take in response to their jealousy feelings also have a serious impact on their relationships.

We think it is helpful to think about *your* behavior as we are describing what jealousy is. When you understand your behavior and what's underneath it, you can begin to take steps to heal it.

We've observed that jealous behavior can manifest in a number of different ways, and what's usually at the bottom is that the person feels fear and does not feel in control.

What do people do to try to control another person or situation? Control can manifest in a couple of different ways. The person who has jealous feelings can lash out with anger or can become very withdrawn and unconsciously use passive aggression to try to control the situation. Guilt can be consciously or unconsciously used in both of these instances.

What happens in both these instances is that walls are built and distance is created. Whichever way is used, the person is consciously or unconsciously attempting to gain control of the situation.

Otto once worked with a woman whose husband was incredibly jealous.

This woman used to talk openly about her relationship with her husband and how painful it was to be with him even though she loved him very much.

She described how her husband would alternate between being angry and out of control one minute, saying awful things to her, and then in the next minute become like a manipulative, little boy who would say things like "Don't you really want to be with me?"

Whichever way he was expressing his jealousy, he was creating mistrust, distance and a lot of pain in their relationship.

Possessiveness: A close cousin to jealousy that also requires some examination . . .

If you are in a relationship where one or both people are very possessive, this can be just as poisonous to a relationship as jealousy itself and here's why…

Possessiveness and jealousy are similar in the respect that underneath possessiveness is either real or imagined fear.

Possessiveness has also got some elements of control mixed in for good measure.

We have over 850 CDs in our music library and as you can imagine, we just love music of all kinds.

Because of this, Otto has always been very possessive about our CD and music collection. He won't loan them out to anyone.

One reason he doesn't loan them is that he's had some negative experiences where he's loaned friends or co-workers albums, tapes or CDs and they've lost them, broken them, scratched them and in one case they were even stolen while someone was borrowing them.

So, as a result, he won't allow any of our music to be loaned out. Period.

But, why does he feel this way?

Where does all this possessiveness come from?

Just like someone who has issues with jealousy, it comes from fear.

Otto won't allow any of the music in our music library to be loaned out because he secretly fears that if we loan out our music that it won't come back.

The fear is that we've worked hard to buy the music in our collection, and no one will take care of it like we will. He's also concerned because some of those recordings can't be replaced at any cost because they're no longer available. He fears that if these recordings get lost, stolen or destroyed that they will be gone forever.

That is the way people who are possessive in their relationships feel as well.

They come from a position of fear and lack. They somehow secretly feel that if they share their partner or friend with others, there won't be enough love, caring, friendship, time, or connection for them.

They feel that they have to do whatever they can to keep control of the other person because if they allow their friend or partner too much freedom away from them, they won't come back.

So, as a result of this fear, the possessive person tries to control the person whom they love, respect and/or appreciate.

But, what we've seen over and over again is that control never works.

When this happens, it only restricts the ease and flow of the relationship. When there is no ease and flow, there is no joy.

When there is only pain and no joy, you are not living the life you are meant to live.

Here's another woman's story about jealousy and control:

"I seem to have 'conquered' my jealousy by looking at it as 'the beast'!!! As I went on in my relationships, I kept aware of that horrible, sickening feeling and fought it by telling myself that I had to conquer that beast. It seems that the problem with this terrible disease stems from our own insecurities. It makes sense when one has conquered it, but at first, it doesn't seem so clear.

"It is so confusing when you are with someone and you have to tell him/her that you don't trust him/her. The other's response is not always going to be supportive so we'd better take care of jealousy before we become involved in a healthy relationship.

"I have done terrible things because of my jealousy but when I finally conquered it and that pain went away, I was able to breathe and enjoy every aspect of the relationship more peacefully.

"So what if your partner looks at another woman and comments on her appearance? So what if your partner speaks to another woman/man at a party? So what if your partner has friends of the opposite sex?

"If you trust yourself enough and don't have that jealous feeling, your partner will open up to you because he/she will be able to be himself/herself. I always remind myself that jealous or not, if my partner wants to cheat, he will, no matter what, but if I become more relaxed with the idea that it could happen and that I AM NOT IN CONTROL, then by showing my trust to my partner, I will show him that I am not trying to control the relationship and by not trying to be in control, I have become more powerful within myself.

"It takes years of practice . . . and sometimes some people trigger jealousy more than others. That sets us back but we have to keep in mind that jealousy is like a disease or a beast. We have to face it, look at it straight in the eyes and fight it until it dissipates and completely goes away . . . hopefully.

"When jealousy takes control of our life, we miss so much of the fun part in the relationship and we create a barrier between our partner and our Self. We create a limitation and no one wants limitations in a healthy relationship. We want to keep growing instead."

Now it's your turn . . .

What does jealousy look like in your life?

What we would like you to do now is take a few moments and describe your challenge with jealousy.

We want you to be as specific as possible. Write down how you feel when you find jealous feelings coming up for you. Write down anything you can think of about specific places, situations, events and even the types of people that seem to be triggers for you that bring jealousy to the surface. Write down your behavior when you feel jealous. What happens between you and the other person?

The reason we are asking you to write down your thoughts and feelings about this issue is that it will help you to become crystal clear about what's really going on in your relationship and life.

You may have been living with this issue for a very long time but the very act of writing it down will help give you a much greater awareness of what's really going on as opposed to what you've been thinking is going on.

Write your challenges around jealousy here:

(Describe exactly what happens when jealousy comes up in your life. Pretend you are an outside observer watching a movie. What do you see? In what kind of situations does jealousy come up for you? Around whom? When? Where?)

_____

_____

_____

_____

_____

_____

_____

The cost of jealousy in your relationships and life . . .

Now, let's go deeper with this idea of describing what jealousy means in your life.

We believe that the first step to changing anything in our lives is to become aware of the pain that some behavior or action is causing. When we have become aware of the cost of the pain, then we can consciously decide if we want to continue to act this scenario out for the rest of our lives.

We invite you to further explore your situation by answering the following questions:

1. "What is the pain that jealousy is causing in my relationships and life right now?"

_____

_____

_____

_____

_____

_____

_____

_____

_____

2. "What pain has jealousy created for me and others in my life in the past?"

_____

_____

_____

_____

_____

_____

_____

_____

3. "What pain will jealousy create for me and others in my life in the future if I do not put an end to it?"

_____

_____

_____

_____

_____

Chapter 2

What Are You Feeling?

One of the important steps to healing jealousy (or anything else) is to discover the feelings that are inside you. In other words, discovering what's underneath the behaviors that have caused you so much pain.

The trick is to honor your feelings as they come up, and yet not let them spill out in unhealthy ways that can ruin your relationships.

Here's an amazing story of what one person discovered after really looking at her feelings and the issue of jealousy:

"I used to be jealous in my relationships including friends and family. After I did a specific training for my career, I learned that people in our lives tend to mirror things about ourselves that reflect a part of ourselves that desire healing. I learned that if someone does something that gets a rise out of us, it is about us and if it does not get a rise out of us, it is about them. It was this learning that moved me forward.

"In a committed relationship with someone, the issue of jealousy came up and he couldn't understand why I became jealous. He gave me no reason to be jealous.

"It was in this relationship that I learned that it was not so much the argument that ensued that was as important as what I got from it.

> *I would ask myself 'How does this make me feel?' As I became aware of the part of myself that desired healing, I became loving and secure in myself and jealousy no longer played a role in my life.*
>
> *"I am now happy for other people's successes and happiness and as a result am able to also receive what I feel for them. Jealousy can be very destructive in any relationship, and the opposite attitude can truly bond families and friends into peaceful and long-lasting relationships that are respectful and caring."*

More about relationships as a "mirror" for what's going on inside you . . .

Mike Wickett is a motivational speaker and seminar leader from Michigan. He has a tape program that we like called, "It's All Within Your Reach," and in it he helps you discover what is possible in your life.

On one of the tapes, he talks about self-esteem and the problems that can manifest when your low self-esteem takes over. He talks about the differences between how he feels about others when he feels good about himself as compared to how he feels about the other people in his life when he's feeling bad about himself.

He said that when he feels good about himself, his wife is perfect and appears to have no faults. But when he's feeling bad about himself, he sees all of his wife's faults clearly.

The truth is that she hasn't changed at all. It's how he's feeling inside about himself that determines how his wife looks in his eyes in any given moment.

If there is jealousy, those feelings usually do not come up because of the conduct of our partner (unless there's a legitimate reason), but rather from ourselves and the way we view our world which is usually from the vantage point of lack and fear.

Many people who we have worked with on their jealousy issues talk about having low self-esteem. They've told us that when they see themselves as lacking, they tend to see their whole world and most everything that is in their world as lacking.

Here's one person's experience with this low self-esteem issue as it relates to jealousy:

"I am a 31-year-old attractive female. As for jealousy, I think what I have goes beyond jealousy. It seems more like an obsession. I have been this way for so many years. I am in my own misery hell. I am learning about it as we speak. I am heterosexual. But I am always looking at other females to see what it is that they have that is better than I. It drives me crazy.

"I have always been told that I am sexy and attractive, but I just don't feel it. It seems that every other woman is MORE attractive and sexier than me. I think being jealous has ruined a lot of my relationships. It is not so much a control thing with me. I just want attention and it seems I need a lot of it. I know I shouldn't need attention from other people, but when your self-esteem is low, you need it to feel good about yourself."

Here's another person's description about how his insecurities make him feel:

"In my relationships with my ex-partners the very destructive emotion we call jealously presided over our ability to communicate. It was like a dark cloud that would release its mighty power whenever and wherever it well pleased. It was ugly, especially when it was exposed for what it was. With a lot of patience and perseverance we were able to determine and agree that our insecurities were based on the hard question, 'Am I good enough?'"

If you want to heal these self-esteem issues or whatever is underneath your jealousy, we suggest that you begin to get in touch with what you are feeling.

Getting in touch with your feelings sounds scary, especially to people who have been taught that certain feelings are unacceptable and encouraged not to show them.

But we've found that it is a crucial step in healing our relationships and ourselves when we begin to bring what we are feeling to the forefront of our attention and just accept that those feelings are there.

One way we've found to be helpful is to stop our busy lives when negative feelings come up and begin to look inward if only for a few moments. Some people call this practice "centering" or "finding your center."

There are many ways to center yourself. You might take a walk or run in a park; sit under a tree; do yoga, tai chi or another form of contemplative movement; or try the exercise that we have included in this chapter. Whatever works for you is okay.

The important thing is to stop your actions and thoughts and to bring your attention into the center of your being so that you can consciously discover what's there.

Here's how one woman used centering to contact what's inside her and to learn to trust herself:

"During my first relationships, when I was much younger, I used to suffer terribly of jealousy, which, sometimes was very well justified. In some cases, it helped me find out that the man I shared my time with was not very faithful. So a little bit of that jealousy helped me see clearly if the man I was dating was worth spending my time with. It was like a test to the relationship. However at other times, my jealousy fooled me and automatically controlled my life. So I decided to work on centering myself more, and learn to trust ME before anyone else. After all, it was my problem, not always the other person's problem."

Getting in touch with your feelings...

If you want to begin to get in touch with your feelings, the best way we know is to do a powerful exercise we've adapted from our friend and teacher Dr. Belinda Gore called the "Power of Presence."

This is a powerful exercise because it helps you to get in contact with what's really going on inside of you. It gives you an opportunity to go within to find out what's underneath your jealous feelings.

The most important thing this practice will do for you is help you to come into the present moment when your mind has already had your partner leaving you for someone else or whatever fears have come up about your relationship.

What we're talking about is a way for you to see things as they really are. No better. No worse. And to help you to shift the feelings that come up to ones that are self-affirming.

Now it's your turn . . .

Here's The "Power of Presence" Exercise . . .

Find a comfortable place to sit, with your back straight and feet on the floor. Close your eyes. Take some breaths and bring that breath into your belly. Slow down and deepen your breathing. When you find thoughts coming into your mind (and they will), simply pull yourself back to focusing on your breathing.

1. The first step is to come into awareness about the chatter in your mind. Don't dwell on your thoughts. Just notice them, pause, breathe and let them go.

2. The second step is to observe what you are feeling about this situation and where you're feeling the jealousy in your body. Are you sad, mad, glad, alone, or afraid? Put an emotion to what you're feeling. Notice where you are feeling this in your body. Is it in your belly area? In your head? In your back? Breathe into that area.

3. The third step is to allow whatever feeling is there to be there. Embrace the feeling and don't try to make it wrong, change it or work on it. Just breathe into that feeling and area of your body and just allow the feelings to be there.

4. The fourth step is acceptance. Bring an attitude of compassion and acceptance to whatever feeling that is coming up. This might not be an acceptable feeling for you but those feelings are there and by accepting them, you are contacting what's inside you.

5. The fifth step is to feel an active presence-to find guidance in your heart by quieting your mind so that you are able to speak and act from a centered place.

Continue to do this until the feeling has no more power over you in this moment.

This is an exercise you can do to be with those feelings without trying to make them wrong, accepting and embracing them without judging yourself.

If you continue to do this exercise when you feel jealous, you will find that the feelings that come up over jealousy will lose their intensity for you.

Here is one of our coaching client's experiences with this presence exercise:

"When jealous feelings come up, I feel this feeling in the pit of my stomach. It feels uneasy. I feel insecure and afraid. I'm not sure why this is happening. It's a false feeling and I need to be able to deal with it. The breathing exercises have helped dramatically to release some of the tension I have been experiencing during these periods. The presence exercise has changed it for me whether I'm alone or with my wife. I still have those false feelings but I'm on the right track.

"The first step is recognition of where you are and that's what the breathing allows you to do. Then you can shift it. The idea is to understand that you're there, then take action to change the physical characteristics of what's going on. By doing the physical changes, you actually release the stress that's going on inside you."

We realize that the reason you are probably reading this material and are doing these exercises is so you or your partner won't *feel* jealous anymore. So giving you an exercise that encourages you to feel but not try to change your feelings seems a bit odd.

But what we have found is that if you bury, try to pretend those feelings aren't there, or deny them, they just come back up as resentment, anger, or some other emotion or action that gets in the way of our connections with other people.

We strongly urge you to practice the "Power of Presence" exercise when jealousy, or any strong emotion, comes up for you, and just see what happens.

One very important way to begin making changes in your life is to stop habitual responses that have tended to damage or ruin your relationships. In other words, interrupt the pattern of "When you do this or this happens, I say or do that…."

The place to begin interrupting the pattern is when you first feel the jealous feelings. Your body will give you clues to help guide you into understanding what is going on and how to stop damaging behaviors.

What's happening in your body?

If you have a hard time identifying what you are feeling, we've found that your body will give you clues to help you discover what's true for you. In our relationship coaching work, we've discovered a very helpful and fairly reliable way to help you begin to understand what your feelings are trying to tell you.

One way to do this is to simply tune into your body sensations when you are doing the Power of Presence exercise. When you are able to do that, a great deal of stress and anxiety can be released by breathing into that area of your body.

We've found that there is usually a direct correlation between the emotion that you are feeling and where in the body you are feeling it.

To get you started looking at feelings in this way, there are three primary areas of the body where feelings and sensations tend to lodge:

      1. the head, neck or shoulder area,
      2. the chest or throat area, and
      3. the stomach or gut area.

For example, if there's discomfort or pain in your head, look to see if you are feeling angry or if you are holding back anger in any way. If you're feeling discomfort, pain or even a tickle in your chest or throat, it usually correlates with sadness in some way. Feelings of discomfort or pain in your stomach area usually mean that there is fear around something.

These are generalities and not hard and fast rules. They are simply possibilities to consider as you begin to make a connection between your feelings and what's going on in your physical body. When you do that, it is much easier to put words to what you are feeling in a way that others can hear them. It's also easier to allow these feelings to pass through your body.

This subject could be an entire course in itself but for the purpose of our work together on jealousy, it's important for you to know some generalities.

It's helpful to put an emotion with where you are feeling a sensation in a certain area of your body to become more aware of what your body is trying to tell you.

With the Power of Presence exercise, plus correlating your feelings with body sensations, we're giving you a way to gain more clarity about how your feelings manifest within your body. We suggest that you use this exercise whenever intense emotions arise. If you do, you'll begin to feel a sense of calm and notice possibilities for your life that you may not have felt before.

Now it's your turn . . .

We ask you to do the Power of Presence exercise again. If you need help identifying your feelings, be sure to use the suggestions that we gave you about body sensations, their locations and the correlating emotion.

Answer the following questions:

1. "When I do the Power of Presence exercise, the feeling or feelings that come up for me around my jealousy are . . . " *(We encourage you to use the five emotions—mad, sad, glad, alone, and afraid—to identify your feelings. Explain in detail what comes up for you when you identify your feelings in this way and use our body sensation suggestions as a starting point.)*

_____

_____

_____

_____

_____

_____

_____

_____

_____

2. "Here's what I am experiencing in my physical body as I feel these feelings . . . "

_____

_____

_____

_____

_____

_____

_____

3. Often we blame our feelings on others. One of the first steps to healing is to recognize that we are the ones creating our own feelings. So with that in mind, we invite you to acknowledge your responsibility for healing.

"I take full responsibility for what I am feeling. No one is making me feel this way." *(Write "yes" or "no" on the line below.)*

_____

Chapter 3

Identifying Your Habitual Patterns

For everyone who experiences jealousy in their relationships and lives, there are habitual patterns that come up again and again that "trigger" jealous feelings.

One way to begin to heal jealousy is to learn to recognize your patterns and identify the triggers that set off those jealous feelings and reactions.

Susie's story:

"Several years ago, I worked at a job where I had to drive an hour each way to and from work. After working eight or more hours every day plus the commute, I usually felt tired in the evenings.

"Although I was tired, I decided to attend a meeting with Otto one evening after work. We had invited Otto's parents for dinner the following day and had planned on going grocery shopping after the meeting so it was a packed day for me.

"After the meeting, Otto was in an intense conversation with a woman for quite awhile, and I found that I was getting very irritated and jealous while I watched them in their deep conversation. Because I was tired, I just wanted to leave the meeting and go to the store to buy the groceries and go home.

"Because Otto and I hadn't seen each other all day, I also found that I wanted Otto's attention. This interaction between Otto and this woman wasn't in any way sexual, but I felt excluded. As a result of how I was feeling, I ended up saying things I shouldn't have and storming out of the meeting.

"Later, when we talked about it, we made the agreement that if I was tired, I would either go home or not go to the meeting at all. I agreed that in the future, I would only stay as long as I was enjoying the meeting and agreed that it was okay if Otto stayed and I didn't. What was also important to me was connecting with Otto, and I agreed that I would ask for time to connect with him if I was feeling a disconnection between the two of us."

Was being tired a trigger or an excuse for Susie's jealousy? Of course her jealous feelings went deeper than her acknowledgment of being tired. The realization that "being tired" and "feeling jealous" were somehow tied together was just the beginning of healing the jealousy that she felt from time to time with Otto and had felt at other times in her life.

In our way of thinking, her tiredness was a trigger that helped uncover thoughts, feelings and beliefs that she hadn't dealt with. By acknowledging that exhaustion often triggered jealousy, she began taking steps to take care of herself and to take responsibility for her welfare. She also began taking steps to heal jealousy in her life.

The point is, that making the agreement to not go to these meetings if she was tired moved Susie to begin looking inside herself for what she was feeling, to come into her center, and to act from what those feelings were telling her.

Now it's your turn . . .

We invite you to wonder about the things in your life that may be triggers for your jealous reactions. With almost everyone there are habitual patterns and themes that run throughout our lives that cause us to react in the same ways over and over again. Keep in mind that these triggers are not the causes of jealousy but may greatly intensify feelings that are already there and bring to light thought patterns and behaviors that need to be healed.

If you consciously make an effort, with practice you can identify what happens in the moment before the jealous reaction gets triggered.

In Susie's story, she was able to identify that being tired often triggers jealous feelings within her.

The beauty of becoming aware of your triggers is that once you start becoming aware of your triggers and you start recognizing them, they seem to dissipate and lose their power and intensity over you.

Here are some questions to ask yourself to help you identify triggers that bring jealousy to the surface and to help you make positive changes in your life:

1. "Is there anything I can recognize in myself that happens when jealousy starts to surface?"

   (Can you identify your triggers, such as feeling hungry, tired, being "stressed out" or overwhelmed?)

   _____

   _____

   _____

   _____

   _____

   _____

   _____

   _____

   _____

   _____

Some examples of ways to help you to "center" and take care of yourself could include:

- Learning to sit and be quiet, doing nothing except breathing for 5–20 minutes per day to center yourself and to lower your stress level
- Having healthy snacks available throughout the day and eating healthy meals so that hunger doesn't take over your emotions

- Cutting down or eliminating stimulants and mood-altering substances from your life—like coffee, alcohol, recreational drugs
- Making sure that you get the amount of sleep that you need each night
- Saying no when you are tired or overwhelmed and giving your body a chance to rest and recuperate
- Taking a walk
- Enrolling in a yoga class

2. "Assuming that there were some triggers, what are some ways that I can begin to take care of myself to lessen the intensity of my emotions?"

(Make sure that you post them in a place that will remind you to do them regularly!)

_____

_____

_____

_____

_____

_____

Chapter 4

The Secret Reasons We're All in Relationships

We'd like to challenge the myth that jealousy is created by one person and that it is only one person's problem.

While we agree that one person in the relationship may have jealous feelings that may or may not have any bearing on the actions of their partner, we believe that both people are participating in the situation. It's what we like to call a "dance" that both people participate in.

Remember the old saying-"It takes two to tango"? Well we believe that this is also true when jealousy comes between two people.

We'll explain what we mean . . .

We believe that the reasons we come together in relationships are to heal, learn and grow.

To some people, these may sound like clinical or dry reasons to come into a relationship. To be connected by love with another human being, to be passionate, to create a family, to have a partner to share life experience-yes, those are all reasons we come together in relationships. But we know that there is more to it than that.

The real reason we all come into a relationship with another person is to experience joy.

When we came together, we knew that there were deeper reasons that we were together and we've found that those reasons unfold every day we are together.

As you probably discovered, everything seems perfect at first when you fall into romantic love. You and your partner enjoy the same activities and seem to speak the same language. You're both on your best behavior, and you are so excited to see each other that you dismiss anything that doesn't fit into this perfect picture.

But after awhile, your partner inevitably turns into someone who irritates you in certain ways, and you wonder why you were attracted to him or her in the first place.

You may even begin to wonder if your partner will be able to give you what you want or need in the relationship.

Well, guess what? We believe that this is all part of why we are together in relationships.

We attract people to us who will act out roles in the play that is our life drama to help us to heal, learn, grow and feel joy. We attract them so we'll hopefully become better people. Unconsciously we find people who resemble one of our childhood caretakers in order to complete unfinished business and to heal old emotional wounds.

Listen to one woman's story about how her childhood influenced her adult relationships:

"Growing up, my father had numerous affairs. I, from a very early age, would notice other girls and women as I got older, and compare myself to them and more often than not, I would find a way that they would outrank me. It could have been their hair, teeth, skin. It didn't matter, there was always something about the other women where some characteristic was better than my own.

"When I was old enough to think about a boyfriend, I always thought that I wasn't good enough because something about someone else was better than I had to offer. Therefore, I was jealous of other women when it came to my situations with men. I became so good at it that I would choose men who wanted other women,

compounding my need to be right about not being able to satisfy a man. In addition to this mess, I was comfortable in it, because I had many years of living in this belief.

"Fortunately, one of my older brothers turned into a wonderful husband and my older sister married another wonderful man, so I did have other role models besides my father. It took many years and even though I'll be turning 50 in June, I still need to remind myself what a beautiful person I am, inside and out.

"The jealousy I experienced was partly due to a childhood experience/memory that took me many years to finally admit and then ultimately address.

"I have been married and divorced twice and find that there's a part of me that can still be attracted to a person who, with charming and charismatic ways, is able to sweep me off my feet only to leave me high and dry.

"I have loving and caring girlfriends, male friends and family, but still I'm working on reminding myself I too can expect a kind and caring relationship with a man who will be true to me."

Susie and Otto's Story:

The two of us have been able to identify the patterns or parts we play in each other's lives. When you start really looking at the relationships you have had, you'll see what we're talking about.

When we came together, it may sound corny but we knew that we were soul mates. We experienced a feeling that went beyond love. It can only be described as a feeling of "coming home."

Even though we felt like we were soul mates, after we had been together for a while, things started happening that caused misunderstandings between the two of us.

In fact, those misunderstandings didn't seem like things that should be happening to soul mates.

We started pushing each other's "hot buttons" and irritating one another. As we worked through these challenges, we were able to gain an understanding about how we were helping each other by being in a relationship together. We began to look at our misunderstandings differently and began to support one another in healing childhood trauma and pain.

What we've discovered is that as children (or perhaps other times in our lives), we weren't able to stand up for ourselves when we experienced emotional or physical trauma. Children (and many adults) often feel so powerless that they hide away the hurts that they cannot deal with at the time it is happening to them.

When we get into relationships as adults, it happens that we attract people who resemble in some way (usually not apparent at first) the person who hurt us in our childhood or perhaps the person who we most wanted to love us and didn't. This person who we have come together with in relationship is giving us another chance to heal this wound that we buried and may have been carrying around for years.

This may sound confusing but maybe our stories will help you understand.

Susie's Story:

"I've had a lot of issues to heal around my father. I always knew that he loved me and he was always there to take care of my physical needs but he didn't know how to access his emotions and tended to keep me at arm's length. I never felt like I could 'please' him and always longed for more of a connection with him.

"I was married to a man for 30 years who at first glance was nothing like my father. When we got married, he was more or less a 'hippie' art student with long hair and beard, the very opposite of my conservative, working-class father. But as the years went by, I began to realize that he was just as emotionally unavailable to me as my father was. Although my first husband loved me and took care of my physical needs, he couldn't or wouldn't connect with me in the way I needed.

"When Otto and I came together, he seemed to be nothing like my father or my ex-husband. But as time went by, I started seeing glimpse's of each of them in some of his reactions toward me. I realized that my relationships with Otto and my ex-husband were opportunities for me to heal the hurts I experienced early in my life. Where I didn't have the understanding or the tools to use my relationship with my ex-husband as an opportunity for growth, I could begin to see my relationship with Otto in a different light and learn from our disagreements and differences."

Recognizing the parts we all play . . .

One of our clients told us that her parents divorced when she was young. She had been "daddy's girl" up until the time he left and she felt abandoned after they divorced. In the past few years, she has often wondered if this abandonment played into her relationship problems. She's educated, holds a great job, and always wants to be the best. She's discovered that she tries to find partners who are needy and ones she can take care of.

What she is coming to realize is that she keeps wanting to be "daddy's girl" again in these new relationships but this time she's playing the part of "daddy" and taking care of her partner the way she would like to have been taken care of.

When you see what part you're playing, then you can stop yourself when you go into these patterns.

Stopping the destructive pattern usually means recognizing that's the way "I" interacted with daddy, or that's how "I" got attention from my mother. It also means realizing how this dynamic has turned into being destructive to your current relationships.

We also attract people to us who have qualities that we think we lack . . .

Another one of our clients, Steve, realized that the women who he attracts have high self-esteem while he doesn't have a high opinion of himself. If a person has low self-esteem, they spend a lot of time beating themselves up. So who do they attract? They usually attract someone who has the confidence they think they lack. They attract a person they can choose to either learn from or someone who will criticize them and validate their low self worth. As Steve realized, we attract people into our lives who will play the roles we want them to play so that we will have an opportunity to grow.

Otto's Story:

"Isn't it amazing that Susie and my first wife are incredibly alike? When I first got together with Susie, because our connection and attraction was and is like nothing I'd ever experienced, I thought she was a totally different kind of person than my ex-wife.

"In some ways she is.

"But, as much as they are different and have traveled very different life paths, there are some striking similarities about both of them.

"What's also interesting is that many of their greatest strengths and qualities are my greatest weaknesses.

"For example: They are both well-educated, extremely organized, focused, task-oriented and good planners. Both have had steady jobs and careers. Not me. Stability is something that hasn't been that important to me up until now. I've held nearly 20 different jobs since graduating from high school.

"Until I learned the power of learning from the people I come in contact with every day, I used to get upset about the fact that my partner was different from me and had different ways of doing things and that she didn't always see things my way.

"Now I understand that nearly every woman I've ever truly been attracted to has had similar qualities. I also understand that I've continued to attract the same type of person to me for a reason.

"That reason is so that I can look at all the characteristics and qualities about them that I am jealous of or wish I had and observe them and learn from them.

"If I'm open to it, I get a great opportunity to heal all the things I find objectionable in myself. I get to do this by just watching the relationship dynamics and dance that goes on between me and the other people I attract into my life.

"Attracting the people that we can most learn from who can help us to heal certain parts of ourselves doesn't just happen in our intimate relationships. It happens in our other relationships as well.

"I'm sure it's no accident that two of the most prominent people in my life, in addition to Susie, have plenty of money and are models of physical fitness.

"I'm sure that this is because I have many things I need to learn in those areas of my life as well.

"One other thought-there is a big reason why these people have attracted me into their lives as well. If they are open to it, they get to expand, heal, grow and learn from me as well.

"They get to notice the qualities in me that they are jealous of or wish that they had and embrace these things into their lives if they choose.

"What we have discovered is that we attract everyone who enters our life for a reason. Sometimes we don't understand right away what that reason is, but it is there anyway.

"My advice is to 'wonder' what you can learn from every relationship and every encounter that comes your way. If you do, you will be much further along the path to creating the life and having the joy that you truly want."

Going deeper with a repeating pattern . . .

Sometimes we think we have healed a certain relationship or situation only to find that it comes around again in the form of a new relationship. This time, if we're conscious about it, we feel it a little deeper, heal a little part of it and are able to let it go a little more.

Jealousy is one of those "hot button" issues that can crop up again and again in your life because you haven't healed some trauma or hurt from your past.

When you and your partner understand that you have chosen each other to heal certain wounds, you can approach your relationship as one that is supporting of both people in their healing process. We've found this healing is one of the keys to happiness.

Strange as it sounds, differences are normal for relationships and conflict can be a way of moving toward healing.

We pair up with people who have issues to heal in alignment with our issues. If your challenge is jealousy, chances are that your partner, in part, has an issue to heal also around that dynamic.

When Claudia was ten years old, she had mononucleosis. She remembers that her mother ignored her during that time and watched television. She carried this hurt with her into all of her relationships, attracting partners who played out this same role. They would ignore her and she would become jealous of them.

In order to heal this issue, Claudia has to keep reminding herself that this is a different situation and become consciously aware of what's happening in her current life. It's a moment-by-moment challenge, but we've found that people can and do move past it.

When both people begin to look at the challenges they face as opportunities for growth-to grow closer and into better people--the dynamic between them shifts from separation to one of cooperation, love and connection.

What to do if your partner cannot or will not see their part in your life drama . . .

Although in many ways, it's easier to heal your "life dramas" if you have a partner who is willing to learn with you, you can begin to shift from jealousy yourself by simply admitting that this is a learning opportunity and to look within yourself to discover your feelings. After you discover and honor those feelings, you can ask yourself what this situation reminds you of and begin to acknowledge that you were hurt. You can begin to learn how to bring yourself into the present moment and know that you are not that person you were then-and that you can become the person you've always wanted to be.

We suggest you begin to look at your partner in a different way: When you come to the understanding that they are bringing up issues and providing the opportunity for you to heal, you can bring more love and compassion for you, your partner and the relationship that will reach into all aspects of your life.

Now it's your turn . . .

Answer the following to discover how your past is affecting you in the present:

1. "When did I first notice jealousy being an issue for me? Did it start in this relationship or in previous relationships?"

(Describe that relationship and situation.)

_____

_____

_____

_____

_____

_____

2. "Is there anything about my current situation and relationship that reminds me of previous relationships or situations?"

(Your jealousy issues may go back as far as your relationship with your father, your mother or any other early caretaker. There might even be a similarity between your parent's relationship and relationships you have had with various partners.)

_____

_____

_____

_____

_____

_____

_____

_____

_____

_____

_____

3. "Are there any patterns that I can see after thinking about past relationships and my current situation?"

_____

_____

_____

_____

_____

_____

_____

_____

Chapter 5

Letting Go of Emotional Baggage from Past Relationships

The first step to letting go of emotional baggage from past relationships is to realize that those old relationships are having an impact on your current life. The challenge is then to stop the thoughts or the "stories" that are being created from past experiences and bring yourself into the present moment.

Todd got a phone call late one night and his partner Mary immediately thought it was his ex-wife on the other end of the line. His ex-wife had frequently called in the beginning of his relationship with Mary and although the calls had stopped, Mary still felt there were feelings between the two of them.

The fear that Todd might go back with his ex-wife stayed with Mary and she just couldn't let it go. In her mind, she worked herself up into a tangle of fear and anxiety as the stories spun around in her head.

Previous to our coaching experience with her, she would attack Todd with accusations and mistrust, but this time she did it differently. As her mind began creating stories about who Todd was talking with, she asked herself the question "Am I 100% certain that the phone call is from his ex-wife?" When she answered no to this question, she was able to calm her fears to a certain extent.

When he walked in the room, she didn't explode with jealous, snide words about who he was talking with, although part of her still wondered. Without being asked, he told her that it was his mother on the phone. Mary had been successful in stopping the stories that she had been creating in her mind and had stopped herself from saying damaging, jealous remarks before finding out who was on the phone. She is learning to reject the stories in her head, to ask herself pertinent questions, to become calm and bring herself into her center.

What a great illustration of first recognizing that there's a story from the past that's going on, and then stopping the story until you know the facts of the situation.

Whether the threat to your relationship is real or imagined, it's the negative stories that spin around in your head that stop you from living in your truth and in joy.

If you experience jealousy, you may be fearful that what you experienced in previous relationships or what you witnessed in your parent's relationship is happening in this current one.

One way to let go of your emotional baggage from the past is to separate out what is true from what is not true and don't let the stories rule your life.

When Otto was in the sixth grade, he remembers sitting in a restaurant, drinking his soda pop, when one of the other kids put his straw into Otto's cup and drank his drink. Today, Otto still unconsciously puts his hand over his cup in a restaurant. The fear is still there somewhere in his psyche that someone is going to put their straw into his cup and take a drink from his cup.

Every time when Otto recognizes what he's doing with his straw and his cup, he has to bring himself back to the present moment. When he recognizes the fear, he lets it go by reminding himself that he is not that young boy anymore.

When dealing with anything in your life and especially emotional issues, the important thing is to separate out what is true and what is not true in the present moment.

One of the most powerful series of questions to know whether something is true or not is from Byron Katie, author of the book *Loving What Is*.

Byron Katie's work is based on four questions that she calls the process of self-inquiry. We've found that these questions can be incredibly valuable in helping you to determine what's real and what's not real.

1. "Is it true?"
2. "Can you absolutely know that it's true?"
3. "How do you react when you think that thought?"
4. "Who would you be without the thought?"

Consider Katie's thought-provoking questions in light of your jealous feelings. When jealous emotions arise, stop, take a deep breath, and do a "reality check" by questioning yourself before you "attack" your partner.

For instance, when Mary was directed to ask herself about her suspicions, she didn't have any evidence that Todd was talking to his ex-wife or that he wanted to be with her and so she knew that she would have to take responsibility for her reaction.

If her answer had been yes, she could have asked herself Byron Katie's second question—"Can you absolutely know that it's true?"

Byron Katie' questions are powerful because they offer tools to help you shift your thinking. If in your mind you've worked yourself up into believing that the person you are with is having an affair and doesn't want to be with you, unless you have specific evidence that your suspicions are true, you have to stop the stories and alter your thoughts.

In our years of working with couples, we've found that a lot of issues will come up when clients consider their reactions. Bringing yourself into the present moment is a term we use a lot to help people step away from the "stories" that keep them stuck in the past.

We can use the presence exercise from Chapter 2 to stop the stories and bring our attention into this moment with this person. We can also begin asking ourselves either Byron Katie's questions or questions of our own like "Is this resonating from truth for me?"

If we use them, these kinds of questions can help us assess what's really going on right here, right now without the baggage of the past clouding the issue.

Here's one woman's story of her path to healing the reoccurring theme of jealousy in her life:

"Jealousy has been an issue not only in my current relationship but in all intimate relationships, whether it be between three friends, or even at work if a colleague talks closely to another person and leaves me out. So I know that the problem comes from ME, from a damaged and wounded heart.

"My partner has been on the receiving end of extreme jealousy with a previous partner which culminated in him having to flee because she was stalking him after they broke up. You can imagine how any suggestion that I may be feeling insecure affects him.

"Potentially we have a recipe for a lot of tension: He is hypersensitive to any probing about his whereabouts, etc, from me and I am hypersensitive to any situation that might trigger an attack. What a nightmare this has been!

"After numerous arguments and getting nowhere, I have looked deep into my heart and decided I can no longer let my fears control me in this life. I consider jealousy like a drink to an alcoholic; it's an addiction. It stirs up feelings which cause the adrenaline rush which gets me high. I get off on the high. It's familiar and makes me feel alive. But it is so damaging.

"If I react to external stimulus, I feed the addiction. If I choose NOT to react then I am taking positive steps to eradicating this monster from our lives. I have decided to practice on a daily basis LETTING MY PARTNER GO. He is free to make his own choices and if he chooses to be unfaithful it is not a reflection on me. If I try to control or monitor him then I suffer. It's like chasing a big monster. I will always lose. I hope we will be together for a long time. Only God knows the plan.

"My conscious effort when the feelings come up is to pray and take 'time out' so as not to nag or question or dump my insecurities on him. This time out is what we agreed on to help me deal with my extreme emotions while I retrain my brain to trust. The moment I handed over my obsession to God, I was on my way to emotional freedom."

Did you notice how this woman recognized that not only was she replaying jealousy in her new relationship, but that her partner had attracted another jealous woman into his life? Neither one of them learned how to deal with jealousy with their previous partners, but she is obviously learning how to move forward in her healing process now.

More tools for healing your past . . .

One way we've found to be helpful in stopping the jealousy pattern is to gently ask ourselves or our partner a question to bring us into the present moment.

In Charlotte Kasl's tape series called "If the Buddha Were in Love," she asks a question that we have used in our own lives ever since we heard it. The question is "How old are you?"

We use it to remind each other when we have drifted into a past story and are acting it out in words or actions but only after agreeing to do so with a loving intention.

The question tends to bring us into the present moment and stop the reactions that are spilling out. We've also found that if one of us is dealing with some issue and it seems that we might be "stuck" replaying some feeling or event from the past, this is a good way to help us break the unhealthy pattern from the past.

If one of us says to the other, "How old are you right now?" the other may think about it and then flash back to age twenty-three or age seven for example. The thought may be "I'm feeling like I felt when I was seven and it's a very familiar feeling to me."

When this question is asked lovingly and with the intention to help, it stops the reaction and allows you to separate the past from the present, bringing yourself into the present moment.

If you admit these feelings are coming from a previous time in your life, it may help you to take a time-out, like the woman in the previous story.

We often say to each other, "I'd like to have a little time and feel what I'm feeling, and then come back together with you to talk about this." These things are not said in an accusatory way but in a kind and loving way.

We take time outs not only when we are in conflict with each other but simply to become clear and calm. When we take time outs, we breathe, centering ourselves, and stopping the mind chatter.

When Otto takes time outs, he likes to sit on the back patio, just sit and be. Other times he likes to take a walk alone.

Susie likes to do a practice called "sitting." In this practice, she just "sits" with her eyes closed, feet on the floor, and breathes into her belly for about twenty minutes at a time. When thoughts come in, she allows them to come in but shifts her attention to her breathing. This tends to calm her jangling, mind chatter that disrupts ease and flow in her life.

We suggest you experiment with these techniques to find out if they work for you. Be open to allowing the past to stay in the past and the present to become more alive and vibrant for you.

Now it's your turn . . .

All of us carry emotional memories from relationship to relationship-some of them more pleasant than others. Sometimes we carry what would be called "negative baggage" from relationship to relationship. If this baggage isn't dealt with and healed, we create "stories" that sometimes have no basis to the reality of our current relationship.

So with this in mind, answer the following questions:

1. "What stories do I create in my mind about jealousy that may or may not have any basis of truth to them?"

_____

_____

_____

_____

_____

_____

Experiment with the ways to stop the stories and bring yourself out of the past and into the present that we discussed in this chapter.

Some ways you might want to try are:

- Taking deep, belly breaths when you are triggered.
- Doing the Power of Presence exercise.
- Asking your partner to help you recognize when you slip into one of the patterns you discovered by asking "How old are you?" or some other agreed upon question.
- Taking a time out.
- Asking yourself "Is this true?"
- Take time each day to do some type of meditation or exercise to calm yourself.

2. "After experimenting with some of the ways to stop the stories, here's how I plan to do to bring myself into the present moment and into my current relationship rather than allowing experiences and stories from past relationships take over my thoughts?"

_____

_____

_____

_____

_____

_____

_____

_____

Chapter 6

Shift Your Attitude from Fear to Empowerment

To begin the healing process that will allow you to eliminate jealousy in your life, you have to take responsibility for shaping your life, shifting your attitude and your focus.

We've discovered that taking responsibility for what we've created in our lives is important to healing anything that we don't want. If our decisions and focus have brought us pain, then making a shift to more positive thinking and actions in our lives will bring us the happiness that we want.

If you believe and know that you can change your life, then you are a step closer to creating the life you want.

Only after you have decided and believed that you can create your life the way you want it, can you begin to shift your focus to what you want in your life-your goals, your dreams, your desires. Shifting your thoughts to what you want will move you one step closer to being the person and having the relationships that you want.

Sound crazy? It isn't. Read the following story and see what we're talking about:

"Learning to trust is one of the hardest things to conquer in a relationship, especially when the trust that had been there in the beginning was violated.

"I was a young girl when I was thrust into the cruel world of cheating, trust and jealousy. You see, when trust is violated by a mate's cheating then the jealousy issue grows. Once a partner has cheated and the trust is crushed, the jealousy is there . . . . all the time. It all goes hand in hand.

"It took me many years to learn to trust again. The journey was long and hard but now I can look back on my life and know that I was only a victim of my youth. Yet there are some people that youth is not always the reason.

"I truly believe now that if you are a jealous person by nature, it has more to do with yourself and how secure you are with yourself to begin with. To overcome jealousy, you first must feel secure in yourself.

"To begin any healing, we all must look inside ourselves for the cure. If you don't want to boggle down your mind with too much information, then try to only absorb this one thing. Keeping this in the forefront of your mind at all times will help you to keep things in perspective. We all must remember one thing . . . We all are at this place in our own lives because of the decisions WE made.

"Circumstances for everyone are different but we all have decisions in life and with each decision, there is an effect. The old cause and effect that we learned in science at elementary school is something that runs through each and every one of us. We chose to go down a certain path and that path led us to where we are now.

"So in order to conquer jealousy, the only thing we can do is to work on ourselves. When we feel secure in ourselves, we no longer have the need to worry about what others are doing. We will be secure in ourselves enough NOT to get jealous. So do what it is that you need to do to feel good about yourself. If that means breaking up with that jerk who points out all your faults then DO IT!!

"It is then that you will begin to heal yourself. Stay away from people who bring you down. Remember, you are allowing them to do that to you. No one else. You are your own best friend. When you finish healing, you will no longer have those jealous feelings."

Just as the woman said in this story, taking full responsibility for your life and shifting your focus to you will help you clear out all those unwanted jealous feelings.

We've found that shifting thoughts away from what your partner is doing or not doing to what you are doing is an important key to letting go of the jealousy dynamic.

If you're obsessed with someone else's actions/behavior, you're not living your own life. We urge you to begin focusing on your life and taking responsibility for creating it the way you want it.

Susie's Story . . .

"I have to admit that sometimes when I was with my previous husband at parties and social functions before we were divorced, I was more interested in who he was talking and interacting with than who I was with. In these situations, I seemed to have one eye and one ear on what he was saying and doing and was not completely attentive to the person I was talking with. I suppose there was a fear that he would find someone more interesting and more exciting than me.

"When Otto and I got together, I found myself doing the same thing with him in certain instances. I certainly knew that my behavior wasn't healthy and knew that I had to do something to shift it. What I did was to begin to consciously place my full attention on the person I had chosen to speak with at these social gatherings. It sounds so simple but when you're trying to break an old pattern, it's very difficult.

"Because I had never had any reason to mistrust Otto, I needed to just deal with me. I had to convince myself that what I was doing and how I was interacting with others was just as valuable and important as what Otto was saying and doing. I had to convince myself that no matter what happened, even if Otto would find someone fascinating to talk to, I was okay and my life was good.

"I came up with some ways that I could help myself feel better and more confident in social situations. I continued my work on raising my self-esteem and with Otto, creating our conscious relationship.

"The important thing that I did was to begin focusing on me and my life, asking myself the question 'What do I want?' and reaffirming to myself that I am a worthwhile person.

"I began to heal my jealousy issues when I acknowledged my fears. This has created more confidence within me and given me greater self-esteem. It has also helped me to start living my life in ways that are more empowering to me."

Making a shift of thought and consciousness

The mental shift of thought and consciousness, like Susie made, can come in many different forms but it always needs to happen for healing to take place.

Here's one woman's story about how she shifted from fear into a more loving, expansive space in her life:

"When I discovered that my estranged husband had been secretly dating another woman, I was devastated. Having just given birth to our fifth child, my hormones and the emergency caesarean had left me vulnerable and weak. We had parted after a series of serious differences, though still maintained intimacy. It was in my heart that he would change and come to live with the kids and me. I knew that the baby would not be the reason that we would come back together. I needed him to see that a part of him had to change.

"When I met his new partner for the first time (I asked to meet her when the truth finally came out), I really wanted to punch her. 'How could she get involved with a man knowing that he had a fifth child on the way?' I asked myself. I scrutinized her and found fault in everything, everything. 'How could he find her preferable to me?' The feelings I let grow inside me were doing me real damage, mentally and physically. I couldn't eat properly for a while and even got rushed into the hospital with a suspected heart attack.

"With determination to get my life right, I had to accept that if I was not going to be with my husband (of twenty-plus years) anymore, I had to get my life back into gear. I sought counseling (Christian Divorce Care) and it helped big time.

"The jealousy side of things, not just his new partner, but the 'wonderful' life they seemed to be enjoying together, was far less of a concern once I accepted that they were both human. It is not mine

to judge. If he is happy then I must be happy for him. Rather than looking at what I was 'missing out on,' I looked at what I had and how good my future was going to be, because it was not meant that I should be miserable, depressed, jealous, etc.

"I let go of the threat that his partner might secretly want to take the baby from me (she cannot have children) and handed her the baby to hold on the first occasion we met. The fear left me the moment I no longer saw it as a threat. Our daughter, who is two and a half now, has a good relationship with her father and his partner and stays over with them one night over each weekend. The other children aged 12 to 18 have adapted to the fact that their mum and dad are not going to reunite. They holidayed with their dad and his partner last year (no threat!).

"The fact that his partner cannot have kids was something I empathized with. I am so lucky I have experienced the joy of motherhood. It is a unique and wonderful blessing. When I see the look on his partner's face when our daughter is around, I understand how she feels, and that joy is something I am happy to share.

"When I was picking myself up, I remember thinking, 'Why feel sorry for yourself and make others sad?' and began meeting my mum at weekends as a social outlet. I focused on cheering her up rather than bringing her down. Through meeting with my mum, I have met a lovely man who I have been seeing for just over a year. I am very happy and exceedingly grateful for the ups and downs in my life.

"I can honestly say that jealousy no longer plays a part in my life. It is my feeling that it is better to be grateful for what we have and look forward to what we can have, rather than get miserable about what we cannot. Also empathizing with another person who is seen as a threat really helps to accept that they are human and entitled to be happy as much as myself and the next person.

"As for fear! All I can say is don't let it come in because it is a destructive force that can put everything out of proportion, and putting out the flames of fear makes for a great feeling inside."

This story is such a wonderful example of how someone can shift from self-pity in a seemingly terrible situation to love and expansiveness. She refused to continue to live in a miserable situation that she realized she was perpetuating by her negative thoughts. By sheer willpower, she willed herself to take steps to let go of her fears and allow love to flow.

So what did it take for Susie and both of the women who told their stories to let go of their fears and move into a more loving space for themselves and for others?

It took accepting responsibility for their thoughts and actions. It took shifting from their fearful, limiting thinking. It took bringing themselves into the present moment and shifting to an attitude of loving oneself and others.

One way we can make this shift in thinking is by using our breath. We introduced you to the Presence exercise in Chapter 2. We use this or a variation of this exercise when we notice negative thinking and uncomfortable feelings beginning to overwhelm us. We sit, we breathe, we tune in. We make a conscious choice to allow the feelings to be there but to also allow a great expansiveness that comes when those negative thoughts have dissipated and the feelings have lost their "charge."

We also begin to actively make goals for ourselves-things that we want very much to do in this life. And then we begin to do them.

Using Affirmations

> *Here's what one of our clients told us about the shifting he was able to experience by using the breathing exercise and affirmations:*
>
> "You need to let go and get in touch with yourself. The way you do that is by the deep breathing exercise. You have and hold in your mind that you want a change in the positive manner. Going through a positive affirmation process is also helpful. Each time I feel jealousy bubbling up, I get in touch by using the deep breathing exercises and know that the things that are coming up are false and have no basis in reality. I affirm that I am looking for happiness, peace, giving and being with my mate."

This person used affirmations to change his thinking and mindset from one of fear to one of possibilities and hope. We like to post affirmations in places where they'll catch our attention throughout the day-like our bathroom mirror, the dashboard of our car, a desk or desk drawer that you open frequently, refrigerator, etc. Be creative but look at the affirmations and say them throughout your day. They may help you to turn your mental chatter around into more empowering, positive self-talk.

Throughout this book, we are giving you some of the tools we use to shift into a more loving, positive space. We invite you to try the ones you resonate with. It takes courage, recognition and moment-by-moment awareness to make the shift we're talking about. Even though this shift may be gradual, the important thing is that you begin to find healthier ways of being in this world and to celebrate when you do.

Now it's your turn . . .

In this chapter, we talked about taking responsibility for creating the life that you want.

Take a few moments and answer the following questions:

1. "What can I do to take more responsibility in my life?"

_____

_____

_____

_____

_____

_____

2. "What are some attitudes, ideas, or beliefs that I need to change in order to move forward?"

(If you're stuck, reread the examples in this chapter.)

_____

_____

_____

_____

_____

_____

Here are a few quotations and affirmations to get you started on creating your own sayings to help you shift into new ways of dealing with jealousy.

"Face your fears and don't be attached to the outcome."
—Susie and Otto Collins

"We can let go of fear when we stop judging and stop projecting the past into the future, and live only in the now."
—Dr. Gerald Jampolsky

"The walls we build around us to keep out the sadness also keep out the joy."
—Jim Rohn

"I am creating my life the way I want it."

"I embrace and appreciate all the love I have in my life."

"I can let go of my jealousy and love myself and my partner."

3. "Some affirmations that I can use are:"

_____

_____

_____

_____

_____

_____

_____

_____

_____

_____

_____

_____

_____

_____

Chapter 7

Creating Conscious Partnerships

One of the positive ways to move forward in healing jealousy is to create trust through conscious partnerships. In this chapter, we'll spend some time explaining what the term "conscious partnership" means to us and how to build trust to create a deep, connected relationship.

We view conscious partnerships in the way that Gary Zukav defines "Spiritual Partnerships." They are relationships where two people come together for their highest spiritual growth. Secondly, in this type of relationship or partnership both partners are equals in all ways.

In a conscious partnership, each person in the relationship commits to growing as a couple and also individually. It is NOT based on any type of religion or dogma.

In a conscious partnership, each person recognizes and knows that the other holds a powerful mirror for them to see past patterns and is supportive in each other's healing process.

They know that they are together to heal the pain of the past and move into a new love for self that spreads to everyone they encounter.

Because the partners support each other in a non-judgmental way, safety and trust are the strong foundation of the relationship.

In a conscious relationship, both people are able to be authentic in who they truly are and are able to speak their truth. Both people are able to be themselves and to speak freely about their ideas and what they are feeling without blame, judgment or criticism. They are simply honored for who they are. In this kind of relationship, both people take responsibility for their actions, their thoughts, and their words.

Sound impossible? It isn't if both people have the same vision, desires and intentions about the relationship.

One of our favorite quotes is by Fritz Perls who said, "Don't push the river. It flows by itself." This is the way it is in conscious partnerships. There is an ease and flow. That's not to say that there are no challenges or "pushing" in a conscious partnership.

When challenges have come up, our commitment has been to tackle the issues as soon as possible so we can regain and keep the feeling of "ease and flow" that is so important to us.

This idea of ease and flow can work for all types of relationships.

Otto has a relationship with a friend that he characterizes as having a great deal of ease and flow. Otto and his friend recognize and honor the differences between them. They don't try to "fix" each other. They help each other when they need it and they allow their relationship to be what it is. They are not best friends but they do support one another. As a result of their intentions for this relationship, there is an ease and flow between them.

Whether it's a relationship between two friends or intimate partners, we've determined that having ease and flow in the relationship is one of the important characteristics if you want to build a deep, connected relationship.

We realize that if you are reading this book, there are probably stresses and strains in your relationship. There probably isn't much ease and flow right now.

Here are some suggestions that we've used in our relationship and other relationships to create more ease and flow that might help improve your situation:

- Appreciate and honor the other's differences.
- Set your intention to create more ease and flow in your relationship.
- Don't try to make the relationship into something that it isn't. Let the relationship be what it is.

- Let go of the need to be right.
- Don't try to change the other person. In order for change to happen, the other person has to want to change.
- Learn to be confident of who you are in your own skin.

Here's how one person describes her relationship with her "soul mate" and how this new relationship helped her to let go of her jealous feelings:

"I was in a long-term engagement and was cheated on. Subsequent relationships ended in heartbreak for me due to a jealousy I couldn't control. I looked at every girlfriend of my other half in a new light . . . What did they do together? and such. It took finally finding my soul mate and love of my life telling me one day. 'I see no one else but you...you are the center of the world and my life' to make me realize that I had nothing to be jealous of.

"Years of heartache and jealousy melted away. I have no fear now...whether he's working after hours with a female coworker or not . . . then again it always helps that when I meet them they tell me I am just as beautiful and wonderful as he has described.

"A lesson to all is the foundation of a good relationship . . . even if it is a loving one . . . is trust. Let go of your emotional baggage from past situations and let yourself free to love and be loved."

We invite you to explore the possibility of creating a conscious partnership with your partner. If you do, we believe that you will experience joy that you've never know in a relationship with another person.

Now it's your turn . . .

In this chapter, we gave you some ideas about what a conscious partnership looks like to us. We hope that that discussion gave you some ideas about what a healthy relationship might mean to you.

In the space below, write down some of the qualities that you want in a healthy relationship.

_____

_____

_____

_____

_____

_____

_____

_____

_____

_____

_____

_____

_____

_____

_____

_____

Chapter 8

Rebuilding Trust

What if you and your partner have significant trust issues, and there are significant problems to overcome before you can begin to create the type of relationship that you want?

In this chapter, you will learn specific ways that you can begin to rebuild trust in your relationship, especially with a person who has violated your trust in some way. If you feel your current partner hasn't given you any cause for the mistrust, you can still use this information to learn to create trust if your jealous behavior has driven a wedge between the two of you.

Several years ago, Otto worked as a door-to-door salesperson for a company in our area. One of the biggest challenges with this job was not so much in meeting the sales quotas but rather to keep from getting bitten by dogs.

One day, less than thirty seconds after a woman told him her dog wouldn't bite, the dog charged after him at full speed. Had the dog's owner not grabbed the dog, Otto would have been bitten.

Because of the way the dog was acting, Otto was skeptical when the woman told him her dog wouldn't bite, and he trusted her even less after the dog tried to bite him!

This is exactly the way it is in our relationships, when someone has disappointed us over and over and we've lost trust in that person. As we've shared in previous chapters, it is also the way we become fearful and wary in our current relationship if we've been cheated on in previous relationships. We just seem to put a question mark in front of everything our partner says or does, even if that partner hasn't cheated on us.

I'm Sorry...

One of the keys to rebuilding trust has more to do with what happens after one or both of you apologizes and says "I'm sorry" than the apology itself.

We've all heard the saying, "Actions speak louder than words" and this is especially true when it comes to rebuilding trust.

When there has been an acknowledgment of wrongdoing or if one person has hurt another in some way, there are some things that both people can do to rebuild trust.

Here's what we suggest for the person who feels they have been hurt:

1. After the apology, be clear about what actions you would like the other person to take to make amends.
2. If the other person is willing, make an agreement about these actions and how this situation will be handled if it happens again in the future.
3. Be open to the possibility that no matter what this person's conduct may have been in the past, this person may change their behavior.
4. Be willing to give up the "victim" position and the desire for making them pay for what they've done.
5. Watch for positive actions by this person in the future and let them know how much you appreciate it when they've "done it right." In other words, offer positive reinforcement.

Here's what we suggest for the person who is apologizing:

1. Understand that a sincere apology is only the first step toward rebuilding trust and your connection with the other person.
2. Ask how you can make amends for what you have done and listen to what the other person is telling you.

3. Be open to the possibility that you can change and get some help if you need to.
4. If you are sincerely willing to change your behavior in the way that the other person suggests, make an agreement to make those changes.
5. Be consistent in your follow through.

Rebuilding trust can take many years or it can happen in an instant. The amount of time that it takes to rebuild trust often depends on how long the people involved are determined to protect and defend their hearts so that they won't be hurt again.

There are many instances when either a person wants to change and just can't or they have no desire to make the changes that will rebuild trust. They just go through the motions and the excuses and apologies are repeated over and over with no positive actions.

If this is what you are experiencing, you have choices to make whether this behavior is important enough for you to take a stand against it or not and if you want to remain in the relationship.

Remember, no matter what has happened up until now, it's always important to give love a chance. It's also important to set healthy boundaries.

Trust in a relationship doesn't start with someone else. It starts with you and how willing you are to open up and allow the other person in.

Now it's your turn . . .

In our discussion of rebuilding trust in this chapter, we gave you some ideas about how an apology can be much more than a simple "I'm sorry." An apology can be the gateway to rebuilding trust in your relationship.

For a look at how apologies work in your life, answer the following:

1. "What challenges (if any) do I have around the issues of apologies and making amends?"

_____

_____

_____

2. "What ideas about apologies would I like to begin using in my relationship?"

_____

_____

_____

_____

_____

3. "What steps can I take to begin to do that?"

_____

_____

_____

_____

_____

Chapter 9

Building Trust with Clear, Honest Communication

How do you build trust in relationships? One of the secrets is clear, honest communication, one moment at a time.

Before we got together, we each came from relationships that simply weren't working anymore. We came to our relationship with the strong desire for a different kind of relationship--a relationship filled with passion, love, honesty, trust, friendship and most of all, partnership.

Safety and trust are the twin sides of the same coin. Both involve risk and both form the foundation of any great relationship. Safety is the feeling you get when you have trust. Trust means not only learning to trust others but it's learning to trust yourself, especially if you've been in less than desirable relationships or painful ones in the past.

From the beginning of our relationship, we've practiced honesty and are committed to not hiding, no matter how painful the truth is.

When you've been used to "sparing" the other person or not saying something because it might hurt their feelings or "rock the boat," it's very difficult to open up and speak your truth. But we believe this is absolutely necessary to form a solid foundation of trust between two people.

Often, people will trust a total stranger before trusting an intimate partner because that total stranger cannot hurt them like they imagine a partner can.

Tony Robbins tells a great story about how we all trust every single day of our lives while driving our cars.

He talks about how much trust it takes to drive down a road at 55 mph with another car coming the other way at 55 mph, often with only a thin, painted line separating the two of you. The potential for danger is great. You don't know that other person; you don't know if they've been drinking; you don't know if they'll stay on their side of the road. Even though those dangers are real, we usually trust that we will be safe.

The challenge is to learn to exhibit the same amount of trust in our relation-ships——knowing, believing and trusting that the other person is acting from their highest good, even if we've been "burned" in past relationships. This trust that we're talking about can only start when you communicate clearly and honestly with your partner, and when you learn how to maintain healthy boundaries for yourself.

Susie's Story

"I grew up in a home where there was a lot of love but we simply didn't express feelings of anger, frustration, and fear. I grew up with the expectation that I should be 'nice' and make everyone in the family feel good. I was not taught to speak my truth but rather hide what I was thinking in order to keep the peace because that's what the women in my family did.

"So in my relationship with my first husband, I continued to hide what I perceived to be my 'negative' feelings. I was often trying to smooth over situations and not express what was really going on inside me, fearful that our relationship would end if I did. I often felt that when I did say what was on my mind, my previous husband would either get defensive and not listen to me or come up with ways to 'fix' it for me.

"Well, guess what? That relationship did end and I would say that it ended, in part, because neither he nor I felt that we could be totally honest with each other.

"We, like a lot of people, believed we were being loving when we withheld perceived unpleasant information from other people, especially each other.

"When I came together with Otto, I knew the type of relationship that I wanted, and that it was one where I could say what I was feeling, and I would be listened to without being judged. In the beginning, we certainly had to practice this new communication style, because it didn't come easily to either one of us."

Otto's Story

"Before Susie and I got together, when things in my relationships got difficult, instead of speaking my truth and saying how I felt about the situation, I would just go along with whatever my partner wanted, just to keep the peace.

"This worked for a while but in the end, I realized that I just wasn't being true to myself. There came a point when I knew I wasn't living my life authentically, and I wanted something more.

"In my relationship with Susie, I am totally committed to saying what I think, how I feel, and what's going on inside for me. This way when I speak my truth, it leaves no doubt as to where we are in the relationship.

"By being completely honest, no matter how painful it is for Susie to hear, I totally eliminate the possibility of miscommunication in the moment. That keeps resentments from building from not saying what is on my mind.

"Most men in this society are taught to 'suck it up' and hide their feelings, doing whatever it takes to please their partner. Popular song lyrics tell us that men had better just say they are sorry even if they don't know why and do whatever it takes to keep women happy.

"For me, speaking my truth as soon as I know it is the only way to create the relationship that I want. What I have found is that if you don't speak your truth as soon as you know it, straight from your heart, it only creates distance and resentments."

Looking inside yourself is the first step

If you want to build trust in a relationship where jealous behavior has caused separation, distance and mistrust, you have to learn to communicate with each other. One of the first steps toward learning how to communicate in healthy ways is to stop blaming each other for the jealousy and to look inside you. It is important that you each take responsibility for your feelings, your thoughts and your actions and take time to discover where the jealousy is coming from.

Maybe your jealousy is because you are secretly fearful that your partner will leave you like a parent did after a divorce, or maybe you got ignored because you were the fourth of five children. Or maybe, you are jealous about the amount of money and the lifestyle that other people have, and you don't think it's possible to have the money you feel you want or deserve.

The point is to stop looking outside yourself for the reason that these issues are in your life. Start looking within yourself for the real reasons that are the root causes of your fears and jealous feelings.

We've given you the Power of Presence exercise to help you discover what's underneath your feelings and we invite you to use this technique and others we mentioned throughout this book.

It's been our experience and the experiences of others that you first have to discover what you are truly feeling before you can communicate it to someone else.

Saying the difficult things...

So, once you know what you are feeling, how do you translate those feelings in such a way that the other person can hear them?

1. Begin with an attitude of curiosity instead of blame and you will see your relationships deepen and grow. Have it as your intention that this other person is your friend and you are approaching this conversation in the spirit of love and not "gotch ya." Approaching conversations to make the other person realize that you are right and he or she is wrong just creates more separation between the two of you. When you approach this discussion with a sense of wonder and with an attitude of "What can I learn from this?" you are demonstrating openness to the possibility of healing your relationship.

2. Create an environment for open communication. We've found that sitting close, holding hands and making eye contact helps to keep our connec-

tion, especially when we have something difficult to say to each other. Although this is the best way for us to communicate, sometimes when we are in the middle of challenges, we have to start out sitting a short distance away from each other but still keeping eye contact. Be sure to turn off the television and park the kids in another room so that the two of you can be present with one another without distractions.

3. Make sure that you have done the Power of Presence exercise or whatever works for you to discover your feelings. It's best if both people can do this, but if you are the only one who does, your communication will go better if you stop and do the exercise before you speak.

4. If communication is a problem between the two of you, it might be a good idea to agree for each of you to have a set amount of uninterrupted time to speak while the other listens. For example, one person may speak for five minutes without being interrupted and then it's the other's turn to speak for five minutes. If you try this, it just might change your relationship forever!

5. Here are a few phrases that we have found helpful that open the door for communication and invite another person to listen to what you are feeling-

"Our relationship is very important to me, and I want to do what I can do to clear up our misunderstanding and the jealousy between us."

"I want us to be able to resolve this issue between us so we can both learn from it and have a close, connected, passionate relationship."

"I'd like to say these things to you and I am asking you to just listen to me and then I will give you a chance to tell me what's going on with you."

By using any of these phrases, you are asking honestly for what you want. You are also building trust that you will each be heard in a kind and loving way. What a gift to learn to give to each other!

6. Be ready to make heart-felt requests about what you would like to have happen in your relationship without blaming the other person. These requests can be specific ways that the other person can help you to feel more secure in your relationship. Make sure you also say what you are going to do for yourself to feel more secure. These requests can also be specific ways that the two of you can rebuild love and trust in your relationship-such as planning a "date night" once a month for the two of you to truly be together.

7. Make sure that you do not interrupt, judge or do anything to shut off the flow of communication between the two of you. Each of you must be given the chance to express what you are feeling. Even if your partner isn't quite on the "same page" as you are with this learning, you will be able to move toward healing the jealousy between you if you communicate what is real for you.

These are just a few of the ideas and ways that we continue to build trust in our relationship by communicating with love instead of fear. We invite you to try them in your relationship.

Now it's your turn . . .

We'd like to give you some practice in translating your feelings into words. In order to do that, we're repeating the Power of Presence exercise as a first step.

Read these directions over a couple of times and then find a comfortable place to sit, with your back straight and feet on the floor. Close your eyes. Take some deep breaths and bring that breath into your belly. Slow down and deepen your breathing.

1. The first step is to come into awareness about the chatter in your mind. Don't dwell on your thoughts. Just notice them, pause, breathe and let them go.

2. The second step is to observe what you are feeling about this situation and where you're feeling jealousy in your body.

Are you sad, mad, glad, alone or afraid? Put an emotion to what you're feeling. Notice where you are feeling this in your body. Is it in your belly area? In your head? In your back? Breathe into that area.

3. The third step is to allow whatever feeling is there to be there. Embrace the feeling and don't try to make it wrong, change it or work on it. Just breathe into that feeling and area of your body and just allow the feelings to be.

4. The fourth step is acceptance. Bring an attitude of compassion and acceptance to whatever feeling that is coming up. This might not be an acceptable feeling for you but those feelings are there and by accepting them, you are contacting what's inside you.

5. The fifth step is to feel an active presence-to find guidance in your heart by quieting your mind so that you are able to speak and act from a centered place.

In order to learn to clearly communicate what you are feeling and what you want, you have to listen to your body, because it is constantly giving you clues. After you have done the Power of Presence exercise, answer the following questions:

1. "Here's what I am feeling, and I'm feeling it in these areas of my physical body."

   (Tune into your body. Where in your body did you feel your feelings? Look for tightness, tension, fluttering, stiffness, pain.)

   _____

   _____

   _____

   _____

Now, put an emotion (anger, sadness, fear) with those feelings. What we've discovered in ourselves and in others who have used this process is that if we do not recognize and express our feelings, they get stuck in our bodies and manifest as pain and discomfort. As we have said before, as a general guideline, the following usually holds true:

- Sensations in your head, neck, shoulders are pointing to anger.
- Sensations in your chest and upper throat translate into sadness.
- Sensations in your navel and stomach area usually mean that you are fearful about something.

2. "I can identify these emotions . . . " (In the space below, write the feeling or feelings that you can identify from your body sensations that you wrote in the last exercise)

Now translate that body sensation and feeling into words:

- "I feel sad about . . . " *(if sensations are in your chest)*
- "I feel angry about . . . " *(if sensations are in your head/ neck/shoulders area)*
- "I feel afraid about . . . " *(if sensations are in your chest) (Remember, no blaming or finger-pointing!)*

3. "I feel _____ about_____

Now that you have a clear statement about what you are feeling, you need to look back in your life to see if you can discover your earliest memory of feeling this way. It may have nothing to do with the problem or challenge at hand, but the feeling will be familiar to you. Answer the following:

4. "I can remember feeling like this when I was _____ years old and the following was going on in my life . . . "

When you are able to connect current emotions with the same feelings you had at other times in your life, you will be better able to heal your current situation and use it as a learning opportunity to move forward. Rather than staying in a place of blame and mistrust, you will be able to say and feel that you want to "do it differently" and you will begin doing so.

If you feel safe enough to share with your partner this information about your past, as well as your clear statement about how you are feeling and what you want, you may be surprised how the communication between you opens up and the jealous feelings begin to vanish. You may find you are able to connect with this person like never before.

Chapter 10

Creating Conscious Agreements

Throughout this book, we've talked about how we have used conscious agreements to help resolve our jealousy and relationship issues. In this chapter, we'll give you some pointers on making agreements so that you can begin creating the love you want.

"Joyce" asked for our advice about her relationship with her partner, the problem being that her partner "Steve" has a close relationship with a woman at work, and Joyce is very uncomfortable with that.

By Joyce's account, Steve spends a lot of time with his co-worker, talks to her about his problems and worries about her welfare. He tends to make light of Joyce's feelings about this relationship at work. Joyce knows the relationship may be innocent, but she is tired of being fearful that they are having an affair and that something deeper may or may not happen between them.

In our judgment, Joyce needs to decide what she wants in a relationship with a partner, find out what he wants from their relationship and then they can begin to create conscious agreements that will work for both of them in all areas of their lives.

If you want to create an outstanding relationship, forming conscious agreements with each other is one of the best places to start.

So what's a conscious agreement?

A conscious agreement defines for a couple what they expect from each another in a given situation. Ideally, you would create these conscious agreements in advance before problems occur. Creating the agreements is not enough. Following through on these agreements is crucial to their success.

Here's how one woman began making agreements with her partner which improved their relationship after a breach of trust:

"We have much more intimacy and trust than before all this happened. It was a painful lesson for both of us. Honest and open communication was key. He had to let me vent and I had to not persecute him constantly. I told him there was no way around the pain and betrayal-except through it. Trust is a fragile thing and it cannot be restored overnight. We both struggled with the trust issue. I gradually relaxed and learned to trust him-but it took time. And, he did a pretty good job of accepting responsibility for his part and understanding my emotional outbursts without getting defensive. Most of all, we communicate our feelings now. When I'm upset, I tell him and why and he agrees not to judge me and take it personally and vice-versa. Honesty wins after all."

Although this woman doesn't use the word, she and her partner did create an agreement. "When I'm upset, I tell him why and he agrees not to judge me." You don't just assume these agreements. You say them.

In Chapter 6, we talked about Susie's jealousy of her ex-husband and Otto in certain social situations. Susie recognized that these were irrational fears and admitted them to Otto. The next step we took together was to create a conscious agreement we could both live with that would help us keep our connection, create trust between us, and eliminate the possibility of jealous feelings before they even came up.

What we agreed to do in social situations, such as parties or large get-togethers, was to connect with each other intermittently throughout the evening by making eye contact or by coming together for a quick hug.

In creating this agreement before the next social event occurred, we were able to talk about what we each would like in those types of situations and how we would like to be treated.

Because of this agreement and the follow-through, the healing of Susie's old issues began and now jealousy is not an issue in these types of social situations.

Most people don't create conscious agreements for how they want their lives and their relationships to be in advance. They might fear that if they begin making conscious agreements in advance, the "mystery" and fun will disappear from their lives.

We disagree because when you don't create conscious agreements, your relationship is ripe for fear, futurizing, disconnection, assumptions and worry about things that may or may not ever happen.

There's another advantage for creating conscious agreements.

Creating conscious agreements is like setting goals in the respect that you are laying the foundation for how you want your relationship and your life to be. Setting conscious agreements helps you keep your relationship on track.

Creating conscious agreements is like setting and achieving goals in another way, too.

When you set a goal or determine that there's something that you want for your life and then challenges come up, you usually don't forget about the goal, start thinking negatively and decide not to go for it.

If what you are doing isn't moving you toward your goal, you usually don't change your goal but you do change your direction for getting there. You come up with new plans and new possibilities for how you can achieve your goal and accomplish what you want.

The point is that if an agreement you make with someone no longer works for you, change it but keep your overall intention for your relationship intact.

Conscious agreements can be changed, altered or renegotiated if they are no longer working or no longer making sense for the two of you.

Another plus for creating conscious agreements is that they can be created for any relationship in any area of your life. They require you to take an inventory of what you want and require you to have the courage to speak your truth with the other person.

Here are a few examples of our agreements for how we want to be with each other and how we want our relationship to be:

- We agree to be best friends and partners: helpers along the way in each other's personal and spiritual growth process.
- We agree to love unconditionally without trying to change the other.
- We agree to tackle issues that come up between us, as soon as we feel distance and disconnection.
- We agree to listen with an open heart, without judgment and without trying to fix it for the other person.

To help you make agreements, here are some ideas that have helped us. We invite you to take what you feel will be helpful to you and combine it with what serves your relationships:

TIPS in forming conscious agreements

- Understand what's at the heart of the problem you are trying to create an agreement about. The problem may not be what you think it is.
- Make clear agreements, not fuzzy ones, that fit your intentions.
- Make agreements in advance of problems whenever possible.
- Try to make agreements when you both are in an open, friendly and connected space.
- Don't make agreements you don't want to do.
- Change agreements when they don't work any longer.
- If one of you or both of you do not keep an agreement, take some time to either recommit to the agreement or to change it.

You may be thinking to yourself that your partner would never go for this idea. If you do have a partner who does not appear to be open to creating agreements, here's how you can find the perfect approach that will work in your particular situation.

For example, if your partner has a reoccurring pattern of being late, first take some time to find out what's at the heart of your problem with his/her behavior. You may want to use the Power of Presence exercise we introduced to you to help you get to the real issue you're having. The other exercises in this book should also help you.

In the example of your partner being late, you may find that the problem is that you desire to spend more time with him/her. (The presence exercise and exercises that go along with it can help you uncover what's really going on.)

After you've discovered the feelings that are underneath this issue, take some time to discover some action that your partner could take that would help resolve this problem.

If your partner is open to it, you could simply express how you are feeling in a positive way and you could both explore what actions could be taken to help the situation.

Even if your partner isn't willing, we suggest you talk with him/her and express what you would like to happen-something positive that wouldn't be perceived as nagging or finger pointing.

A good approach is to ask for his/her help with a problem you're having.

Find a time when you can be alone without any distractions such as the television, computer or children and say something like this-"You know what I'd like? I'd love to spend more time with you in the evenings. Maybe we could begin taking walks like we used to or even start riding our bicycles again. Would it be possible for you to start coming home at 6 pm a couple of nights a week, and we can plan some dates (or time) together?"

If he/she agrees that that's a good idea, follow up by planning dates for the nights that have been agreed on. Be proactive in following through on making your agreements work. You might want to write them down and post them somewhere so you both can see them.

We've found that when you take the approach of asking for what you want in a positive way, your chances of getting it are certainly increased.

We urge you to begin to create agreements for the way you'd like your relationship to be. You may be surprised by what happens.

Now it's your turn . . .

After reading this chapter, you should have a good idea of how to create and negotiate agreements to help heal the jealousy in your life.

Now it's your turn to actually create some agreements with your partner, if possible. If you don't have a partner or if your partner is unwilling to create agreements with you, we invite you to create agreements for yourself about how you would like to be in your relationships and in your life.

Complete the following: (If you are creating agreements with a partner, you should each answer questions #1 and #2 separately and then discuss your answers before you complete #3 and #4.)

1. "A situation I would like to create an agreement around is . . ."

_____

_____

_____

_____

2. "I would like these ideas to be in this agreement . . . "

_____

_____

_____

_____

3. "I (we both) agree to the following . . . "

_____

_____

_____

_____

_____

_____

_____

_____

4. "Some ways we (I) can remind ourselves (myself) of this agreement are . . . "

_____

_____

_____

_____

_____

_____

_____

Chapter 11

Opening to Possibilities

One of the most important ideas we can offer is to open yourself to new possibilities in your life. By reading this book about jealousy, you have begun the process of becoming aware of your situation and what is possible in your relationship and in your life. We invite you to begin today to move out of your feelings of hopelessness to trying some of the ideas and techniques we've given you.

We live in a 130-year-old house and every now and then a bat will find its way in. When we first came together and a bat would decide to make its appearance in the house, we would haul out the "bat tools" (which consisted of a tennis racquet and a shoe box) to try to get rid of it. The bat extraction always involved a lot of shouting, chasing the bat and drama.

Now, when a bat gets lost in our house, we adopt a more humane and painless way of helping the bat find its way out. We just turn on the outside lights and open the door. Usually in just a few minutes, the bat realizes that the door is open and it just flies out.

We feel that this change of attitude and approach to getting bats out of our house can also apply to healing jealousy and becoming more open to love and possibilities in your life.

Not only is the change of attitude important in this story but also the symbology of the "bat" itself gives us clues to healing our challenging situations.

In many cultures and traditions, the bat (the night-flying mammal) is considered to be a symbol of rebirth, transition and initiation.

In the book *Animal-Speak* (a book about animal symbology) Ted Andrews writes, "Most people fear transitions, holding onto a 'better the devil you know than the one you don't' kind of attitude. If a bat has flown into your life, then it is time to face your fears and prepare for change. You are being challenged to let go of the old and create the new."

Healing jealousy requires you to face your fears, let go of the old, allow changes to happen and create something wonderful and new.

One of the biggest reasons that people don't have great relationships is that they don't believe it's possible-that it happens to someone else and not them. Just like the lottery--someone else always wins and they don't.

We're here to tell you that love and the relationship you want is possible, and you can have it if you open yourself to the possibility.

If you want to create outstanding relationships, do what we did: spend your time wondering about possibilities instead of focusing on what you don't have and have never had in your life. We both focused on the possibilities of having the love we've always wanted. And that's what we continue to do in our lives.

When there's disharmony and disagreement between us, instead of allowing ourselves to be shut down and disconnected for long periods of time, we focus on the possibilities of opening to each other and regaining our connection.

Is this easy to do? No, it's not easy.

Essential to a great relationship? YES!

No matter what is going on in your life and in your relationships, we suggest that you be open to possibilities instead of shutting down in the face of fear. It isn't always easy to do but the rewards are enormous.

So how do you begin to be open to possibilities?

Take baby steps and celebrate them

You begin by taking baby steps-one step at a time-and celebrate them!
How many of us recognize and celebrate the progress and growth we've made in our relationships and in our lives, even if they are baby steps?

As we were thinking about our own relationship, we realized that when challenges come up between the two of us, we are now spending less time being disconnected from one another, whether it's from jealousy or any other fear-based problem.

When challenges come up, we are finding our center and regaining our connection much quicker than we did a year ago. We are also being a little less defensive with one each other and every time, we do a little better at speaking what is true for us and feeling safe about doing it.

On the surface these may seem like small, inconsequential things. But, when added up, they result in a significant impact on the quality of our already outstanding relationship.

Remember, even small changes do make a difference.

We invite you to look for the positive "baby steps" as you begin your healing process. Focus on possibilities and what's going "right" in your relationship rather than what is going "wrong."

Take some time to share with your partner and celebrate what is "right" or good in your relationship and ask your partner to do the same.

Focus on what you want

Essentially, we're suggesting that you take some time and intentionally focus on finding the good in yourself and in your relationship.

This is important because very often people spend a lot of time focusing on what's going wrong in their relationships and not on what's "going right." They spend a lot of time focusing on jealousy or any other challenge but not on the love that is or once was between them.

In life and in your relationships, whatever you focus on, you attract more of. We're suggesting that if you want more joy, connection and love in your life that you spend more time focusing on these things than the things you want less of or want to eliminate.

This is a simple, yet powerful message that most of us know but forget. Everyone knows that when we have positive thoughts and give positive feedback to those in our life, everybody feels better.

But what do most of us do? We continue to dwell on negative thoughts and give negative feedback to our loved ones.

Many years ago when Susie's daughter was in school and she brought home her report card with mostly excellent grades on it, Susie would find herself commenting first on what her daughter could improve upon instead of complimenting her on doing a good job.

In these instances, a great opportunity for connection was missed because Susie focused on what her daughter could improve on instead of what she was already doing well.

In the past few years, accentuating the positive is something we are trying to consciously incorporate into our lives and it can definitely help your jealousy issue.

Since Susie does most of the cooking, she appreciates it when Otto calls to let her know when he will be late for dinner. When he calls, she tells him that she appreciates his call. She gives him an "attaboy" instead of complaining that he's going to be late or that the dinner will be ruined.

Otto getting an "attaboy" for calling to say he's going to be late has a much more positive effect on him than if Susie would have said, "Late again?" or "Dinner will be ruined!" or "What are you doing that you are late this time?"

This is just one small example of something that we both do on a regular basis. It improves the quality of our relationship and builds trust between us. We are constantly telling each other how we appreciate the value we each bring to the other's life.

So you might be asking--What do you do if you can't find anything that you appreciate in your partner? What if there isn't anything positive that you can find in your relationship?

No matter how bad a relationship is, there has to be something positive that you can catch the other person doing so that you can begin to show your appreciation. That's where you start-wherever you are. That's how you build a great relationship—one moment at a time.

We've learned that if you focus on the negative, that's what you'll get more of. If you focus on the positive, that's what you'll attract into your life.

Three little words that can change your relationships and your life...

You're about to discover a simple three-word phrase that has the power to change your relationships and your life forever.

This phrase is "Up until now . . . "

To us, these are much more than three little words strung together. It's a philosophy of hope and possibility. It's also a way to remind ourselves that the past is over and we can always create our life anew starting right now.

This "Up until now . . . " philosophy also means that no matter what mistakes you feel you've made, challenges you've had or problems you've encountered along the way, today is a new day and anything is possible from this moment forward.

If jealousy has been an issue for you in all of your relationships or even if it's just appeared in your current relationship and you feel stuck and don't know what to do, it may sound simplistic but you do have a chance to do it differently from this moment forward.

Whether you're twenty, thirty, forty, fifty or eighty years old, it's never too late to begin again.

So, how do you do this?

Step one is to acknowledge for yourself that there are other people who have exactly what you want for your life and to adopt the belief that if it's possible for someone else, then it's possible for you too.

Once you begin to believe that yes, other people do have what you want and it's possible for you too, then begin opening yourself to opportunities that will come your way.

Don't beat yourself up if you fall into old patterns that don't serve you. Simply recommit to creating the life or relationships that you want.

If you feel that you must talk to others about your disappointments about the way things have been in the past, always use the phrase "up until now . . . "

By using the phrase "up until now . . . " you are opening your heart and mind to possibilities that are waiting for you.

Now it's your turn . . .

As a final exercise, we invite you to answer the following:

1. "What is going right and what do I appreciate about my relationship and my life?"

_____

_____

_____

_____

2. "In what ways can I show my appreciation to others in my life?"

_____

_____

_____

_____

3. In what ways can I use the phrase "up until now . . . " in my life?

_____

_____

_____

_____

Final Words...

We hope that you have gained some insights in how to begin your healing. By reading this book and doing the exercises, you have demonstrated openness to a new way of being in relationships. We encourage you to take our suggestions and begin using the ones that resonate with you on a regular basis.

We wish you much success in your healing process and if we can help you further in any way, please contact us.

Blessings to you,

Susie and Otto Collins

Websites:
www.NoMoreJealousy.com
www.RelationshipGold.com
www.collinspartners.com

Email:
info@collinspartners.com

Phone:
(740) 772-2279

Appendix 1:

"No More Jealousy" Worksheet

Copy this worksheet and use it whenever you are feeling jealous. It will help you come into the present moment, discover what's underneath your feelings and help you heal.

Keep copies of this worksheet handy so that you can refer to it when jealousy appears. We also suggest that you keep your answers in a prominent place so that you won't forget that there is a way to resolve jealousy in your relationships and in your life.

1. "My thoughts and feelings of jealousy in this moment are . . ."

_____

_____

_____

_____

_____

_____

_____

_____

_____

2. "This current situation reminds me of what happened in these past rela-
    tionships and in these times in my life . . . "

    _____

    _____

    _____

    _____

    _____

    _____

    _____

    _____

    _____

3. "After thinking about my answers to #1 and #2, what's REALLY under-
    neath my jealous feelings and thoughts is . . . "

    _____

    _____

    _____

    _____

    _____

    _____

_____

_____

_____

_____

4. "I am staying stuck in my jealous feelings by acting or thinking in this way
   . . ."

_____

_____

_____

_____

_____

_____

_____

_____

_____

_____

5. "A new way I can think and act in these situations is . . ."

_____

_____

_____

_____

_____

_____

_____

_____

_____

_____

6. "I can remind myself to try these new ways when jealousy comes up for me by . . ."

_____

_____

_____

_____

_____

_____

Appendix 2:

Tactics and Strategies for a Jealousy "Emergency"

What to do if your situation is a true jealousy emergency . . .

If you are reading this book right now, there's a chance that you are in the middle of a full-blown jealousy crisis or emergency.

We define a full-blown jealousy crisis or emergency as:

A situation where one or both people in the relationship are having either current or consistent challenges with jealousy and these challenges are creating major problems in the relationship to the point that it is in jeopardy.

For the person having the feelings of jealousy and anxiety: It could be that you are feeling overwhelmed, not knowing what to do, and not making sense of your relationship and your life to the point that you are fearful that if you don't do something, you will ruin the relationship.

For the person in a relationship with someone who is extremely jealous: You may be finding yourself wondering how much longer you can take the accusations, fear, drama and control. You fear that if the jealousy isn't healed and healed quickly, you may no longer want to be in this relationship.

You also fear that if the jealousy isn't healed and healed quickly, the erosion of trust and pain that you both are experiencing will be so great that the relationship will not be able to survive.

If something like this is happening in your life right now, we've written this for you.

When there is a major jealousy crisis in your relationship, what you do next determines whether you can and want to rebuild trust in the relationship or whether you and your partner should design a plan to leave the relationship with grace.

What are your options when you're in a true jealousy crisis?

When there's a true jealousy crisis, you only have three choices:

1. Stay stuck. You and/or your partner hold on to your fears, blame, judgment, being a victim, and stay trapped with jealousy for as long as you are in this relationship and even after it's over.

2. End the relationship. You and/or your partner acknowledge and accept how big of an issue jealousy is in your relationship and decide that you cannot stay in this relationship because the pain between the two of you has been too great.

3. Heal the relationship. You and your partner acknowledge and accept how big of an issue jealousy is in your relationship, look at your situation openly and honestly, and consciously decide that your relationship is important enough to commit to doing whatever is necessary to healing the jealousy issues.

Which option will you choose?

If you decide to hold on to your fears and feelings of blame and judgment, and to stay shut down emotionally, it will be impossible for you to heal the jealousy and start repairing this relationship.

On the other hand, if you (and your partner) are both willing to open your hearts more, make the commitment to do whatever is necessary, it is possible to heal jealousy and save the relationship, no matter how bad your situation appears to be right now.

In this section, we'll outline some proven and powerful action steps that you can take to begin to rebuild trust in your life when there have been major jealousy issues between the two of you. Whether you are the one who feels victimized by actual acts that your partner has done or if you have carried your pattern of jealousy from relationship to relationship and it's threatening to destroy your current relationship, these steps will help.

If you have any possibility of rebuilding trust, you have to act and you have to act soon. You cannot sit idly by and hope that your relationship will repair itself. It will not! This is not a time for excuses, withdrawing, retreating or dealing with it another day.

If a major jealousy crisis is underway in your relationship and you want to regain trust that's been lost, you have to begin taking positive steps toward healing it now.

A word of caution . . .

If you are in a physically, emotionally or sexually abusive relationship and/or drug or alcohol addictions are involved, your first step is to stop the abuse and the addictions. Before addressing your jealousy issues, both people usually need to get help to stop abusive or addictive behaviors and to learn how to be in relationships differently. So if this is you, get help now for yourself.

In the following sections, we're offering specific suggestions for three specific situations that make up jealousy emergencies:

1. The person who is jealous and their partner has done nothing to "deserve" the jealousy

2. The person who is the target for jealous behavior of another person but they have done nothing to "deserve" it

3. One or both people have done things to break trust in the relationship and one or both people find it difficult to trust each other again

This section is written for the person who is jealous when it appears that their partner has done nothing to warrant their jealous behaviors.

If this describes your situation, here are our suggestions:

1. As quickly as possible, take some time for introspection. Take a walk, take a few minutes alone, listen to some soothing music and in short, do whatever you can to calm down and reduce the intensity of your feelings. This doesn't mean that you're going to hide your feelings and pretend they aren't there.

If you are not thinking clearly and are feeling anxious and overwhelmed, then breathe deeply in your belly in order to begin placing yourself in a space where you are clear and your intense emotions are not clouding your thinking.

2. Before you approach the other person in this relationship and attempt to repair the damage that you have done with your jealous behaviors, it is important that you take some time to acknowledge to yourself what you have done to create this situation and search for repeating patterns of this behavior in your life. As you are doing this, find out what is going on within you and find out what you are thinking and feeling.

    Make sure that you read the book and work through the questions that we've included, because you will find many strategies to help you identify where these feelings are coming from that are triggering the jealousy.

    Use the Power of Presence exercise in Chapter 2 of this book to help you get clear on what you are feeling.

    Ask yourself this very important question:

    "Am I willing to commit to doing whatever is necessary to resolve these jealousy issues within myself and rebuild trust between the two of us?"

    If you answer yes to this question and really mean it, healing jealousy and rebuilding trust is possible if the other person is also willing to make the commitment to rebuild trust.

    If your answer is no, then the prospect of healing your jealousy and rebuilding trust is dismal.

    Until you are committed to looking at the thoughts, feelings and fears that are underneath your jealousy, there is usually no chance of a successful reconciliation because you will just repeat the behavior again.

    So, take this time of introspection to truly decide where your thoughts and behavior originates and whether you can commit to doing whatever is necessary to help yourself heal. That may mean finding a therapist or coach who will help you resolve some of the hidden issues that are underneath your actions.

3. Create a written statement of your commitment.

    If you have decided that you want to try to heal jealousy and rebuild the trust that's been broken and are willing to do whatever is necessary, make a written commitment to yourself that this is your intention. Anything less than total honesty at this point will be of no value to anyone.

4. Commit to asking for forgiveness and making amends for your jealous actions and behavior.

    Saying or thinking that you are "sorry" will probably fall well short of what is necessary to rebuild your relationship. You have to ask for forgiveness and explain what you are going to do differently in your relationship.

    To do this, you will need to begin using the strategies that we teach in this book to heal your jealousy, moment by moment when jealous feelings arise.

    Make a list of what you are willing to begin doing to make the changes in your life that you know that you need to make.

5. Ask the other person to talk with you about this situation.

    If this is or has been an explosive situation or you have repeatedly falsely accused him/her of being unfaithful, it may be a challenge to get the other person to listen to what you have to say. Expect that the other person may have a lot of anger toward you and may want to tell you about how badly they've been hurt. Try to listen and understand where the other person is coming from and admit what you have done.

    After hearing the other person, this (or something like it) is what we suggest you say and do in order to take the first step in demonstrating your commitment to healing jealousy and rebuilding trust and this relationship: (Do this only if you are sincere about it!)

    Tell the person that you are totally committed to healing jealousy, rebuilding trust and repairing the relationship and that you are willing to do whatever is necessary in order to do this. Ask them how you might begin doing this and then listen to what they have to say.

If the person will not talk with you, you can write a letter and tell them that you take responsibility for what you have done and tell them how you are going to change. Then take steps to make those changes whether the person will talk with you or not. If you will begin to make positive changes in your life, you will find that all of your relationships will improve even if you may no longer be in this relationship.

6. Listen while the other person talks and don't get defensive or interrupt. The person may need to rehash the situation and let you know "again" how much you have hurt them. Allow them to do this and don't interrupt. If they seem to be repeating themselves without telling you what you can do to make changes in your relationship, we suggest that you acknowledge the pain you have caused and ask them directly what changes you need to make. Tell the other person what steps you are willing to take to make the changes you know you need to make. Be specific.

7. There are some things to consider before you commit to making the changes that are being asked of you and that you want to make yourself. Make sure that you have the desire and belief that you can actually follow-through to making the changes that are required before you commit to the other person.

Before you commit to making the changes that you are agreeing to make, consider if you are truly committed to doing it. If the changes that you need to make seem overwhelming and you have doubts that you can do them, you will need some type of support system to keep you on track to help you keep these commitments. These might include a coach, therapist or a family member or friend.

You may need help and support in changing your behavior and that is why we are suggesting that you seek the help of a support person, counseling, or coaching.

Your partner may ask you to learn more effective ways to communicate. Taking a class or reading a book may give you the support that you need to begin learning new skills to help you make the desired changes.

If you are asked to make changes that you don't want to make or cannot make, be up front and honest about it. Make changes for yourself and not for the other person.

9. Ask if your partner wants to rebuild the relationship.

   Ask him/her the following question (or something like it), "If I can demonstrate to your total satisfaction that I am willing to change, are you willing to commit to doing whatever is necessary as well?"

   The answer this person gives in response to this question will tell you whether they have it in their heart to forgive you and whether they have the desire or not to rebuild the relationship.

10. Make your agreements and commitments in writing and post them where you will see them. Keep them in your purse, pocket, desk drawer or car- anywhere you can see them often. Take them out and read them anytime you are falling into your old habits of jealous reactions.

11. Keep your agreements and commitments.

   There is no other way to change except to keep your agreements and commitments, one moment at a time. Be predictable in your behavior. If you do, it will help your partner to see how far you've come in this process of healing jealousy.

12. When doubts and insecurities come up within you, if you are sure that these fears are false, instead of getting into another painful discussion about specifics, try telling your partner something like this: "I'm feeling insecure right now, would you just hold me close and look in my eyes so that I can feel your love."

If the two of you can't get past the damage that jealousy and mistrust has created in the relationship and this relationship dissolves, don't give up on making the changes that you know that you need to make. You've probably learned a lot from this process so take this knowledge and apply it to all your relationships in your life, both now and in the future.

This section is for the person who is the target for jealous behavior of another person but they have done nothing to deserve it.

If this describes your situation, here are our suggestions:

Remember the choices given to you at the beginning of this chapter?

We'll repeat them here so that you can get a clear idea of where you stand.

1. Stay stuck. You and/or your partner hold on to your fears, blame, judgment, being a victim, and stay trapped with jealousy for as long as you are in this relationship and even after it's over.

2. End the relationship. You and/or your partner acknowledge and accept how big of an issue jealousy is in your relationship and decide that you cannot stay together because the pain between the two of you has been too great.

3. Heal the relationship. You and your partner acknowledge and accept how big of an issue jealousy is in your relationship, look at your situation openly and honestly, and consciously decide that your relationship is important enough to commit to doing whatever is necessary to healing the jealousy issues.

While we believe that it's very healthy to acknowledge the pain that a person has caused you when unwarranted jealous accusations are made, it's not, however, healthy for you to stay stuck in that pain.

Staying stuck does not allow movement toward rebuilding your relationship or in letting the relationship go. It keeps both of you in limbo.

Letting go of staying stuck is a conscious decision.

So, with that being said, your first challenge is to decide which of those choices you are going to take. If you choose to move forward, it doesn't have to mean that you want or will be able to be in a trusting relationship with this person. It only means that you are not going to stay stuck.

If you choose to move forward, here are some suggestions to help you to decide whether you are open or not to considering rebuilding your relationship:

1. Calm down. You are not going to be thinking clearly if you are extremely angry about your partner's jealous accusations. Breathe deeply in your belly in order to begin placing yourself in a space where your thinking isn't clouded by intense emotion.

After you are fairly calm, take some time to get in touch with what you are honestly feeling about this person and this situation-not what you *should* feel but what you are actually feeling. If there's anger, hurt, or fear, allow those feelings to be there and simply acknowledge them. Use the Power of Presence exercise in Chapter 2 to help you honestly assess if and how you might be able to move forward in this relationship.

Fear is not always a bad thing. Sometimes fear can be a wise counselor, signaling what you need to look at in your life. Fear can also keep us from moving forward. As Thaddeus Golas said in *The Lazy Man's Guide to Enlightenment,* "We think fear is a signal to withdraw, when in fact it is a sign we are already withdrawing too much."

2.   Look at your part in this relationship "dance" to discover how your thoughts and actions could have contributed to this situation. This doesn't mean placing blame on yourself for what has happened between the two of you. It means honestly looking at your relationship and how there may have been things that you could have done differently, for example, speaking up to say what you wanted instead of withdrawing, or being more loving with your partner.

3.   Get clear about what you want.
     A vitally important question to ask yourself at this point is-"If my partner (the person you are in relationship with) is willing to change their jealous behavior, do I want to stay in this relationship with them and give it another chance?"

If you can honestly answer this question with a positive yes then rebuilding this relationship is possible.

If you get a no when you ask yourself this question, then you'll have a clear message that too much damage has been done between the two of you for you to open your heart once again to create a better relationship.

No matter which answer, being honest with the other person is your best course of action because it will either move you toward the healing process or move you into dissolving the relationship in the least painful way. Being honest also helps you to see the relationship for what it is and helps you and your partner to know what will truly be possible in this relationship.

Some people stay stuck in dead, lifeless relationships for many years because they aren't willing to be honest with themselves and each other.

If you are honest with each other, you will reduce the amount of time that you are stuck in pain.

If you said yes to this relationship and the possibility of starting again with this person, here are some suggestions to help you do that:

1. Before you speak to the other person about this situation, get clear about what changes you would like in the relationship. What evidence would you have to see in the behavior of this person so that you would know that he/she has changed? What actions would you like this person to take to make the changes that you want in your relationship?

2. Consider what it would mean to forgive this person and to move past this current situation. What steps are you willing to take to help you to begin the forgiveness process? Forgiveness may not be something that you are willing to do right now, but realize that whatever the situation, sooner or later, for your own health and well-being, it is something to work toward. Without forgiveness, you cannot create a healthy relationship between the two of you.

3. Have the courage to share with this person, openly and honestly. This may simply mean that you will agree to listen as this person tells you what they are willing to do differently in your relationship, and then you share how you are feeling and what you'd like to have happen. Or it may mean making the first move to communicate with this person.

    If you are making the first move, as soon as you are clear about your feelings about this situation, seek out this person and share with them that although you are hurt and in pain, you are willing to be open to the possibility that the relationship could be healed if certain things happen.

4. Share what you are willing to do to make the relationship different. Accept your role or responsibility in what has happened in the relationship and accept the possibility that there were things that each of you could have done differently. Take responsibility for your own empowerment by

accepting your role and actively choosing some positive ways to move toward the relationship that you want.

How do you want to be different in this relationship? Are there some new skills you want to learn either by yourself or with your partner to help make the relationship better? You may want to consider counseling or coaching, either by yourself or with your partner, to help you to create the kind of relationship that you both are wanting.

Are there ways you can support your partner as he/she learns to let go of jealousy as a way of life?

5. Make written agreements that you both can live with and keep.

6. Keep your agreements; be willing to let go of the past and start fresh in this relationship. Stay in the present moment. When you find yourself slipping into negative thinking about your relationship and dredging up old hurts, remind yourself that this is a new day.

This section is for the couple where one or both people have done things to break trust in the relationship and one or both people are finding it difficult to trust each other again.

If this describes your situation, here are our suggestions:

1. Both of you take the time to calm down. Breathe deeply in your belly in order to begin placing yourself in a space where you are clear and your intense emotions are not clouding your thinking.

2. Take some time for introspection, discovering what you want in this relationship. This probably means spending some time by yourself. How much time you need to spend in introspection and thought is totally up to you. Some people need only a few minutes to get clear about what they want in their relationship and other people might need hours or even a couple of days.

    In our opinion, if you spend any longer than this in reflective time, you're either avoiding the situation or you need help from a trained therapist or coach to help you get clear about why you appear to be stuck or unwilling to say yes to yourself and speak your truth in this relationship.

If you do choose time by yourself, tell the other person when you would like to talk.

As you remember, at the beginning of this section of the book, we told you that there are only three choices for how you can handle jealousy and this relationship.

To help you discover what you want in this relationship, we're repeating those three choices here:

> 1) Stay stuck. You and/or your partner hold on to your fears, blame, judgment, and being a victim, making your life and your partner's life miserable.
>
> 2) End the relationship. You and/or your partner acknowledge and accept how big the separation is and how much pain is between the two of you and decide that you no longer wish to be in this relationship.
>
> 3) Heal the relationship. You and your partner acknowledge and accept how big the separation is between the two of you, look at your situation openly and honestly, and consciously decide that you are committed to doing whatever is necessary to heal the relationship.

3. If you are committed to doing whatever is necessary to heal the relationship, create a written statement of your commitment. It may mean asking for forgiveness and making changes in your life if you have done something to destroy trust in the relationship. It may mean looking honestly at your part in whatever happened to destroy trust, even though you may think you are the victim. Look beyond the immediate cause of your separation and into how you could have been a better partner.

4. If you were the one who created the situation that caused the two of you to mistrust each other, commit to asking for forgiveness and making amends for your behavior. Saying or thinking that you are "sorry" will probably fall well short of what is necessary to rebuild trust in a relationship crisis situation. You have to ask for forgiveness and make changes, not based on what you think is appropriate, but on what the person you have wronged thinks and feels is appropriate.

5. If you are the one who is the "victim" and you now find that you are exhibiting jealous behavior when you never have before, take some time to discover what changes you want in your relationship, assuming that

your partner is willing and wants to make amends for what he/she did.

6. The only way to make amends to another person for something one person has done is to first find out what changes the other person wants and then both people ask themselves what will make the relationship better. The only way to find out what these changes are is to ask. In this situation, what you think is appropriate may not be enough or may not be what the other person thinks would be "right" from his/her point of view.

7. Take some time and talk with each another about the situation. Each person should take turns talking and listening to each other without getting defensive or interrupting. (Difficult but important to do) This may be a challenge if one person is very hurt and angry. The person who has "caused" the mistrust needs to listen and to try to understand where the other person is coming from and admit what he/she has done to cause the pain. Both people should realize that the problems with the relationship did not start with the actions that caused this current separation.

8. Each person should talk about how they would like their relationship to be and what changes they are willing to make to have it. If one or both people are stuck in blame, it's impossible to create trust again. Both people need to be willing to look honestly at how they want their relationship to be in the future and what it's going to take to get there.

9. As always, if you need help from a professional, get it. Changing behavior is not always easy, and it's very helpful to ask someone to support you in this process.

10. Make your agreements in writing and post them where you will be reminded of them.

11. Keep your agreements and commitments. The only way to do this is one moment at a time. Be predictable in your behavior. If you do, it will help your partner to see how far you've come in this process of rebuilding your relationship.

12. If one or both of you are more interested in punishing each other than rebuilding the relationship, then you have a choice to make if you want to stay in the relationship or not. Know that if this happens, you can still make positive changes in your life and learn from what happened.

About Susie and Otto

Susie and Otto Collins are married relationship and life success coaches from South Central Ohio who spend their time sharing with others how to create more conscious, connected and loving relationships and lives.

Together, they are the authors of books, tapes and over two hundred published articles on relationships. Their book titles include: *Should You Stay or Should You Go? Creating Relationship Magic, Communication Magic, No More Jealousy, Creating Relationship Trust, Attracting Your Perfect Partner,* and *The Relationship Attractor Factor.*

For thirty years, Susie has been a student of relationships, spirituality, energy and the life force. Her search for physical, emotional and spiritual healing has led her to the study of Polarity Therapy, cranio-sacral therapy, reflexology, Hatha Yoga, the Enneagram, and much more. Her formal training includes a Bachelor of Science degree in education and a Masters degree in Library Science. She is a Registered Polarity Therapy Practitioner with the American Polarity Therapy Association and a certified comprehensive coach. Susie is a veteran teacher and university librarian with over thirty years experience teaching in the public schools and university classes.

On the university level, she's taught courses in Education, Communications and currently teaches a Women's Studies course.

Otto has spent over twenty years as a successful salesperson and marketer of a variety of products and services. Many years ago, as a result of pondering three of life's greatest questions-"Who am I?" "Why am I here?" and "What's this all about? -- Otto turned his life's focus to bear on the practice and study of spirituality, personal growth and relationships.

Susie and Otto's formal coaching training has been primarily from The Hendricks Institute and Comprehensive Coaching U. For well over twenty years, both Susie and Otto have immersed themselves in the study of personal and spiritual growth, with their primary focus being the study of creating outstanding relationships of all kinds. They continue to share what they have learned through their books, audios, web sites, workshops, seminars and their daily lives.

They passionately believe that life can be lived in a joyful, conscious, loving way and are committed to helping others to experience the potential of what is possible in their own lives and relationships. The desire to be loved the way they wanted to be loved took each of them on a journey of discovery of how to create the relationship of their dreams. They believe Spirit put them together for their own personal growth and to shine the light of hope for others. Their goal is to help others create outstanding lives and passionate, alive, connected relationships.

They write a free weekly online, content-rich newsletter that offers proven, practical tips and ideas for solving relationship problems and challenges that reaches well over 30,000 people in over forty-seven countries. They speak from their own experience and what they have learned from their relationship coaching practice clients, teaching people how to create relationships that last and ones that are filled with joy, passion, connection and love.

Contact Info

For more info about working with Susie or Otto personally to improve your relationships and have them be your Relationship or Life Coach, call them at (740) 772-2279, email info@collinspartners.com or visit www.collinspartners.com/relationships/coaching.htm

Susie and Otto Collins
P.O. Box 1614
Chillicothe, Ohio 45601

"FREE Relationship Mini-Course"

*"Discover Susie and Otto Collins' Amazing Secrets
For Creating a Closer, More Connected and Loving Relationship!"*

Sign Up For Our FREE 5-Day Email Mini-Course:

This Course Will Teach You..

- What is the #1 way to improve communication in your relationships?

- What are the secrets to getting what you want in your life and your relationships?

- How can you master the most important relationship skill you need to develop?

- How can you build more trust in your relationships?

- How can you say what you want to your partner in a way that it can be heard?

Get this FREE Relationship Mini-Course by visiting . . .

www.FreeRelationshipCourse.com

Susie and Otto Collins' Relationship Books and Courses

The Relationship Attractor Factor
A simple 7-step process that anyone can use to attract
and keep the love they want. For more information, visit:
www.RelationshipAttractorFactor.com

Should You Stay or Should You Go?
Susie and Otto's break-through process for helping
anyone make the best decision possible about whether
to stay in or leave a relationship.
For more information, visit: www.StayOrGo.com

Creating Relationship Magic
In this e-book, Susie and Otto have identified 52 of the biggest
challenges and issues we all face in our relationships. They show
how anyone can create magical relationships in their lives.
To find out more, visit: www.CreatingRelationshipMagic.com

Creating Relationship Trust
Of all the qualities that make up a good relationship, trust is
undeniably the most important. Discover the relationship secrets
for building trust and dramatically improving your relationships.
Visit www.relationshiptrust.com

Communication Magic
How to immediately improve communication in all your
relationships and to create a lifetime of love.
Visit www.communication-magic.com

Printed in the United States
211100BV00002B/1/A

9 780972 513081